THE NEW ANTIQUARIANS

THE NEW ANTIQUARIANS

WRITTEN & CURATED BY

Michael Diaz-Griffith

PRIMARY PHOTOGRAPHY BY
BRIAN W. FERRY

MMXXIII

INTRODUCTION—8
The Persistent Richness of Things

CHAPTER I—14
Emily Adams Bode Aujla & Aaron Singh Aujla

CHAPTER II—32
Adam Charlap Hyman

CHAPTER III—50
Pablo Bronstein

CHAPTER IV—68
Alex Tieghi-Walker

CHAPTER V—84
Jeremy Simien

CHAPTER VI—98
Giancarlo Valle & Jane Keltner de Valle

CHAPTER VII—108
Jared Frank

CHAPTER VIII—122
Camille Okhio

CHAPTER IX—132
Collier Calandruccio

CHAPTER X—146
Kyle Marshall

CHAPTER XI—160
Sean McNanney & Sinan Tuncay

CHAPTER XII—176
Abel Sloane & Ruby Woodhouse

CHAPTER XIII—190
Emily Eerdmans

CHAPTER XIV—204
Jared Austin

CHAPTER XV—220
Avril Nolan & Quy Nguyen

CHAPTER XVI—234
Samuel Snider

CHAPTER XVII—248
Andrew LaMar Hopkins

ACKNOWLEDGMENTS—268

TO THE AFFECTIONATE MEMORY OF
PHILIP HEWAT-JABOOR

in gratitude for his encouragement of
"grown-up" collectors of all ages

Introduction

The Persistent
Richness of Things

If a story begins with finding, it must end with searching.

– Penelope Fitzgerald, *The Blue Flower*

Three of anything makes a collection, but a collecting practice can be ignited, quietly, by a single bewitching object. This book honors that inaugural object and the nascent collector's first step, taken perhaps unknowingly, into a lifetime of desiring, studying, searching, and only occasionally, when the conditions are just right, finding.

A great number of young people are taking that first step today, and the images and stories in these pages demonstrate that young collectors do indeed, despite fears to the contrary, exist. I call them the New Antiquarians, not because they uniformly collect antiques—some collect vintage material, or a mix of antique, vintage, and contemporary art and objects—but because they follow, with considerable spirit and rigor, in the long, eccentric tradition of treating the practice of connoisseurship as a serious vocation. Some of the New Antiquarians are connoisseurs already, while others have progressed well down the path to becoming such. All are passionate about objects and their histories, and they have convinced me, over the past decade, that the future of historic art, antiques, and the material culture of the past is in good hands.

Why should it be otherwise, you might ask? Like romance, the collecting bug takes hold of us before we know to doubt it, and any student of history will conclude that human beings will always be, according to their nature, acquisitive. Still, in recent years, those in the know—

antiques dealers, curators, seasoned collectors—have prophesied an extinction event for collecting. To understand why, we must cast our glance back to the closing decades of the twentieth century.

Between the 1970s and early 2000s, the market for antiques and historic art ascended to precipitous heights, adding untold value to the world's store of old things. Entire categories of objects that had been considered unfashionable or even objectionable, from English furniture to American folk art, returned to vogue, along with the practice of collecting itself. Volumes could be dedicated to the economic and cultural reasons for this boom, and undoubtedly some would strike a negative tone. The period, especially the 1980s, has been characterized as an Age of Excess. For collectors and connoisseurs, however, it was a Golden Age. Objects were not just desired; they were violently contested and victoriously won, from the sharp-elbowed aisles of antiques shows to the increasingly glamorous auction house floor, which became a locus for public spectacle. There was little doubt that things mattered, and no question at all that stewards would volunteer themselves, perhaps too readily, to usher them into the next century—paying millions of dollars, if necessary, for the privilege of doing so.

The problem with booms is that they are pregnant with busts. So it was with this boom, which slid into a downturn around the turn of the century before busting, with barely a whimper, after the financial crisis of 2007–2008.

What happened? Did the recession cause collectors to tighten their belts in the usual fashion, or did the trouble go, mysteriously, deeper? Some gestured to the specter of 9/11 and the endless wars that followed, murmuring about a generational shift from beauty to survival. Others pointed to the burgeoning taste for minimalism among Gen X, or those born between roughly 1965 and 1980, which produced a mania for midcentury modern at a time when the material was still too new, despite its vintage status, to be seen through the lens of continuity rather than disruption. Meanwhile, at the bottom of the market, IKEA rose to a status first of ubiquity, then of hegemony, becoming a kind of shorthand for everything antiques lovers hated: flatness, convenience, and above all, disposability.

Historians of these times will marvel at our obliviousness to the internet's rise, even as it remade our world. While the antiques market cratered, the vast jungle gym of high society began to fail, too, reducing the stakes of socially competitive activities such as collecting, decorating, and dressing. To some it seemed the whole art of living was under attack, and certainly it was in abeyance. After three hundred years of decreasing formality, Western households embraced casual lifestyles and open floor plans, foregoing dinner parties in favor of gatherings around the kitchen island or aggressively disaggregated happenings around the house. AOL Instant Messenger did not require the use of hats, gloves, and stoles. It barely required the use of a chair.

At the height of the antiques boom, by contrast, an ambitious couple on the Upper East Side could be expected to own a set of eighteenth-century dining chairs in the manner of Thomas Chippendale or John Linnell. Their counterparts in Kansas City might have acquired clever reproductions of relatively recent manufacture—not because they could not afford originals, but because there simply were not enough to go around. In Alabama, where I was born and raised, overpriced nineteenth-century imitations or "cheap and nasty" modern reproductions (to borrow a phrase from William Morris) would have exuberantly filled the same gap.

Thirty years later, however, few cared if you had a dining room or not, and the chairs gathered around your table (if you had one) were immaterial to your social existence (if you had one). In a digital age of ultimate plurality, one style was as good as another. If you collected, with few exceptions, it was for love of the thing itself.

Against this backdrop, the grande dame of the antiques world, New York City's Winter Antiques Show, soldiered on. When I joined the fair in 2015, eager to help dust it off, I found that the pinnacle of the antiques market had stubbornly refused to collapse, or its collapse was slow enough to evade detection by the naked eye. Sometimes, late at night, I suspected the latter. Serious Discussions were convened, and over glossy conference tables and glasses of Champagne it was agreed that masterworks would always be in demand; institutions and the very rich would continue paying good money, as they are designed to do, for the best. But what of everyday collectors— the kind who might buy a set of chairs for their dining room? Would there appear a new wave of moderately wealthy, eccentric, or foolhardy enthusiasts ready to offer themselves up at the altar of collecting? Sometimes my colleagues looked to me, the lone twentysomething in the room, to answer this question. Sometimes they did not.

I found both responses to my presence highly motivating.

As I walked around the fair's event for younger people, begun in the nineties by the children of board members, I ran a sort of diagnostic test through gimlet eyes. I had attended Young Collectors Night before, but as a guest pursuing my lifelong hunt for art and objects of fascination. Now, on a different mission, I surveyed a troubling scene: cash-fattened bankers accompanied by mysterious beauties in red dresses; stands abandoned by their exhibitors and, like crime scenes, cordoned off from visitors; and a provisional DJ booth, vibrating with tinny sound, that doubled as a drop-off for drained drinks.

Dealers referred to the proceedings as "The Young and the Checkless," and I understood why. No one was buying. Of even greater concern: few were looking. The Upper East Siders who cochaired the event huddled together, making the most of their unwieldy creation, and on paper their party was a success: it raised desperately needed funds for the show's charity beneficiary, East Side House Settlement, a community-based organization in the South Bronx. It did not reflect a new wave of interest in anything, however, much less historic art and antiques. Quite the opposite. Here was the bust on display for all comers to see—or anyone with $200 and a Thursday evening to spare.

The good thing about busts is that they are pregnant with booms, and happily I sensed a boom brewing in other quarters. Millennials had begun retaining, rather than dispossessing, inherited heirlooms, and dredging affordable treasures from overlooked reefs of unwanted objects. Nostalgia was in the air. On the still-novel digital app Instagram, people of all ages discovered a dematerialized temple of beauty, posting—and feverishly discussing—obscure historic interiors, works of art unearthed in newly digitized museum archives, old photographs of vintage fashion, and objects of every description. On Tumblr, the youngest people alive—the world's first "digital natives"— assembled collections of history-related ephemera, some of it ironizing (on-set shots of Kirsten Dunst, in costume as Marie Antoinette, taking a smoke break) and some of it earnest, even academic in scope. At Gucci, the Italian fashion house known for its sleek, nocturnal brand of glamour, creative director Alessandro Michele was beginning to engineer one of the great turnarounds in fashion history, devising a complex new set of codes for the house derived, with an impish gusto that grew each season, from historical references. It came as no surprise that his Instagram account enjoyed cult status; it was, like an increasing number of others, a panoply of gently decaying palazzi and idiosyncratic personal collections. For even more palazzo porn, lovers of beauty could subscribe to *Cabana*, a biannual bible of soulful interiors layered, invariably, with collections. Later, as Michele's star waned at Gucci, other collector-designers rose in the firmament: Jonathan Anderson, creative director of Spanish fashion house Loewe, featured a king's ransom of Rococo candlesticks from the mid-1750s in an advertising campaign that went viral among Very Online antiquarians.

Meanwhile, at the monthly shelter magazines, editors once again commissioned stories featuring ruffle-and-bow-bedecked interiors. At fashion presentations on the Lower East Side and London, young brands—Batsheva, Bode, Palomo Spain, Puppets and Puppets—embraced historical references, too, and those presentations soon became Fashion Week–sanctioned runway shows. In the arts and pop culture, figuration and gestures toward the Old Masters proliferated, from the work of artists such as Kehinde Wiley and Salman Toor to Beyoncé and Jay-Z's "Apeshit" music video, which was part homage, part institutional critique of the art-historical complex. A spirit of retro-postmodern play moved through the realm of collectible design, then the culture at large, followed by a kooky wave of neosurrealism and the arrival of "medieval modern," a Gen Z–meets–Axel Vervoordt expression of historicist minimalism. Everywhere, it seemed, everyone spoke of craft—that is, the old ways of making things by hand. With mounting excitement, I cofounded a connoisseurship-focused affinity group for young collectors in 2018, the New Antiquarians, and documented the vibe shift on my Instagram account. Where else?

None of this resulted in a sudden change of fortune for the world's store of old things. Antiques and historic art were returning to favor as references, but collecting has never been a young person's game, and for good reason: it requires disposable income. Free-spenders and the childless enjoy a head start, with young parents and the financially prudent following behind as money allows. As we freshened up the Winter Show and turned around Young Collectors Night, and as I began working with galleries, auction houses, museums, magazines, and other fairs, helping them stoke—and prepare for—this burgeoning wave of interest, a cynic would occasionally challenge me: "Where," gesturing around, "are the new clients?" A dealer once insisted he would not engage with younger people until they proved themselves worthwhile by beginning to buy, making the first move in the courtship dance that is the dealer-client relationship. He wanted, he said, to be wise. I understood his reticence. Quite possibly he owned a warehouse of unsold material from the time before the bust. But wisdom has its limits. One day soon the pendulum would swing, bust would become boom, and we would wake up in a new world.

We live in that new world today. Young collectors do indeed, despite fears to the contrary, exist, and this book is evidence of their existence. At antiques shows and auctions, these New Antiquarians not only look, but buy. Online and in these pages, they share their collections—considered, here, in the context of their homes. They do not collect due to social pressure; they collect for love of the thing itself. While some hail from families with a collecting gene, others, including myself, began collecting ex nihilo. In a digital age of ultimate plurality, we are choosing the material culture of the past, or it is choosing us. For collectors of color, queer collectors, and first-generation collectors, that choice—or calling—can be freighted with complexity, but it is also charged with possibility. Collecting is a tradition, but an eccentric one, and it is carried out most capably by freethinkers who prize self-expression, the pursuit of an individual sensibility, and the discovery—often through old things—of the new.

As you will see in the pages to follow, the New Antiquarians do the new as well as the antique. Some mix or display objects in new-fashioned ways, while others reclaim or recontextualize history through the things they have chosen to steward and interpret. A few, brilliantly, do all of these things at once. In their collections and stories, it is my hope that you will find surprise, delight, and inspiration for your own collecting practice.

Finding, after all, is only the beginning of the story. Once you've been bewitched, the search begins again—for more objects, for their true nature, and for your own, poised restlessly between the future and the past.

Mexico City
December 1, 2022

I

EMILY ADAMS BODE AUJLA & AARON SINGH AUJLA

Chinatown, New York City

Handmade dollhouse furniture, American quilts and linsey-woolsey coverlets, Alsace pottery, Bengali literature, senior corduroys, and vintage Chanel.

Among collectors, there are those who collect objects as objects, fixated on the particularity—the thinginess— of each thing they acquire. These objects could land in a private gallery, a hoarder's heap, a storage facility, or any other place where a thing can be visited and beheld, cradled, and considered. At the end of each visit the door can be shut, the box can be closed, and the object can be trusted to retreat, unseen, into its auratic singularity.

Then there are world-building collectors like Emily Adams Bode Aujla and Aaron Singh Aujla, for whom objects are the material of life, not discrete things to be collected in isolation. In the designers' Chinatown loft, each object tells a story, reflects a craft tradition, reveals a personal reference, or participates in a ritual of everyday life, and most—as far as I can see—perform all of these actions at once, in dialogue with each other and their stewards, and in harmony with the purpose-built environment that houses them all.

If Emily and Aaron were not designers, the world they are building, object by object, would simply be that of their apartment: a complex, Cape Cod–meets–Chandigarh cosmos swirling above Lower Manhattan. Designers they are, however,

and prolific ones at that, and the world they are building, project by project, has no known edges.

For Emily, a preservationist to the bone, history is alive in the present, and our emotional connection to the past—down to its most mundane processes, such as mending worn textiles—imbues contemporary life with a richer meaning. It is no coincidence that the seasonal collections for her fashion brand, Bode, are autobiographical in scope. When viewed together, they amount to a vast scrapbook of memory derived from her own life, the lives of family and friends, and the lives of objects she has known. On sourcing trips, I imagine Emily neck-deep and deeply happy amid mounds of antique and vintage textiles at the Brimfield Antique Flea Market, or rummaging through dusty but perfectly preserved trousseaux in Provence: cutwork, bobbin lace, unused bedsheets, and monogrammed napkins, all ready to be documented, aired out, and circulated back into life.

In her world, a supply of deadstock fabric may be sewn up into new clothes, tailored for future memories but charged with an ineffable feeling for the past. A particularly precious textile, on the other hand, might be archived, studied, and reproduced by Bode's artisans and tailors, requiring them to learn—and thus preserve—extinct (or nearly so) craftways in the process. This is preservation in its truest sense, running through objects as well as the hands that make them.

Of course, an object might also be kept at home, accessioned to a growing collection. This is where Aaron enters the frame. Like a nineteenth-century curator, respectful of objects but particularly sensitive to their aesthetic presentation, he is responsible, as often as not, for the placement of Emily's finds. The couple's collaboration at home mirrors their work together, although detecting the hair-thin boundary between life and work, with these two, is a fool's errand. Over a decade ago, Emily influenced Aaron's shift from the fine arts to the realm of furniture design and interiors; meanwhile, Aaron and Benjamin Bloomstein, his partner in the research-based design studio Green River Project, a sort of literary-historical think tank with saws, helped conceive of Bode's immersive, narrative-driven presentations. In recent years, building on those ephemeral displays, they conjured the growing brand's numinous tobacco-stained-and-scalloped stores. Like the built environment of Bode and the apartment pictured here, Green River Project's quarterly collections begin with a set of Bauhausian parameters that are dizzyingly upended, or sharply clarified, through engagement with historical references from tramp art and natural history museums to the films of Satyajit Ray.

Old, but with a sense of futurity. New, but with a sense for the past.

For those concerned with the display of *things*, Emily and Aaron's apartment could be a model for the private gallery in our post–white cube age, drenched in mustard-yellow paint and suggestively screened as it is, yet formally clarified enough to serve as a showplace for objects. Even so, it is not a place where a thing can be visited and beheld, cradled and considered, and then put away. There is no door for shutting or lid for closing. The objects on display are immanent and everywhere, and the material of life spreads all around.

Previous: In the living room, everything is vintage, antique, or made by Bode or Green River Project. The sofa was inspired by a craft tradition started by Purdue University seniors in 1904, when they began elaborately decorating yellow corduroys in the manner of yearbook pages. Emily collects—and reproduces—senior cords today. Scrawled dialogue from a Satyajit Ray film imprints Aaron's sensibility on the sofa. A rare note of irony is sounded by a pastiche of Picasso's *Figures on the Seashore* (1931) by artist Matt Kenny.

Opposite and right: The couple's wood-and-window-lined bedroom revolves around a screen put into service as a headboard. It is hung with a Picasso print from the 1960s. Personal talismans fill the sanctum sanctorum: the lamp belonged to Emily's paternal grandmother; the quilt was a gift from a trusted textile dealer; and the bedside table, rich with markings, hails from dealer, interior designer, and friend Michael Bargo. The vintage journal atop the table features a cover design by filmmaker Satyajit Ray, one of Aaron's guiding spirits.

Page 26: Of all the spaces in Emily and Aaron's apartment, the bathroom feels the most transportive, perhaps because it was the only room to be conceived entirely from scratch. There is also something thrilling, as a visitor, about finding collections where you least expect them. Here you find dried plants, antique Indian figurines, a headless stone sculpture from the couple's friend Michael Bargo, and a collection of Raja Ravi Varma prints. Light floods the space, and an unobstructed view of Lower Manhattan feels hopeful, somehow.

Right: An abiding appreciation for memory, family, and the integrity of materials runs through Emily and Aaron's lives and design practices. In their kitchen, stainless steel, plywood, Douglas fir, and Formica conspire to create a demotic kind of magic, and an unpretentious setting for kitchen tools—and domestic rituals—inherited from family. If superficially luxurious fittings tempt you, study this photo closely. The true makings of luxury are here.

Opposite: Alabaster grapes test the limits of mimesis, and a Raja Ravi Varma print commands the attention of all comers.

Above: Wooden parrots from Emily's mother watch over the kitchen. Above is a blue Lachenal tea set. On the pegboard are the implements of everyday life, left right out in the open, including an ice cream scoop from Emily's paternal grandfather. Why not buy a pegboard for yourself and hang your collections from it? Julia Child would be proud. I suspect that Emily and Aaron would be, too.

II

ADAM CHARLAP HYMAN

Midtown, New York City

Victorian majolica, Aesthetic Movement furniture, Eastlake picture frames, shell-adorned objects, Italian ceramics and Radical Design, and theatrical illustrations from the 1920s and '30s.

As children, we hold seashells to our ears and listen to the ghostly resonance within. For some, this is the sound of the sea, or the shell's memory of the sea from which it has been parted. For the ancients, who saw in shells a symbol of fertility and eternity, and a conduit to the gods, their obscure music may have suggested another realm altogether: a mystery beyond human knowledge.

It should come as no surprise that shells feature prominently in the work of architect Adam Charlap Hyman, which derives from a scholarly yet synthetic understanding of art history, an unusually rigorous interpretation of modernism, and a keen sense of the lowercase-*s* surreal—that is, the sphere of dreams.

In less exacting hands, these influences might produce a chaotic brew, yielding rangy, overgrown fantasy gardens dotted with oddities or infinite interiors piled high with the strange and unusual. In Adam's world, however, gardens are of clipped yew and rooms are discrete, and each object they contain glows with a talismanic power that illuminates its own mysterious nature. Here there are few answers, but mysteries present themselves forthrightly, amplified by the spiraling walls of Adam's genius.

In such a practice there can be no meaningful boundary between collecting, designing, and dreaming, but that does not make it an unserious one. Rather, the opposite is true: "I am interested in *things*," says Adam, a hardened connoisseur at the age of thirty-two, "and in what we know and do not know about them." I imagine a future for Adam as a serial collector of the obscure disciplines that fascinate him: Victorian majolica, papier-mâché furniture from the reign of Napoleon III, 1970s Art Nouveau Revival glassware, objects rendered in the form of things they are not (seashells, asparagus, hands). Yet, try as I might, I cannot produce an image of Adam, Collector, among his trophies. If he owned a thousand Japanese prints, I am certain he would find a distinct home for each one, hung high against the ceiling or leaning against the baseboard, each print in precisely the spot that allows him—and us—to appreciate its auratic, thing-y particularity.

As a world-creating sandman, of course, he designs these spots with expansive punctiliousness, and the Midtown Manhattan apartment pictured in these pages can only be seen as a Gesamtkunstwerk. When I spy the verdant Madeleine Castaing–designed carpet of Adam's bedroom through a crack in the door, a passionate sense of anticipation grips me. Stepping inside, I see that he has placed atop the carpet a nineteenth-century painted table, an echo of Castaing's taste, and my anticipation is rewarded a hundredfold. Atmospheres, too, can be collected.

There is inevitably another, deeper layer: a through-the-looking-glass headboard by artist Katie Stout has just been installed above Adam's striped daybed. Studded with fever-dream fruits, flowers, mushrooms, snails, and, yes, seashells, its crowning glory is a conch—separate from, but related to, the rest of the composition, mounted high above the room like an amulet.

"I think this space is close to being right," Adam says with characteristic sincerity. "I can't see it looking any other way, you know?"

He pauses to locate, in his way, the most precise and humble expression for what he is about to say, and I sense that it will be the most important thing I hear all day. I am not wrong.

"Everything," he says, gesturing to the objects around us, "is beginning to sing."

In his voice I hear the echo of the seashell.

Page 38: In the playful front hall, examples of contemporary design arranged in a rhythmic composition beckon visitors inward. Only the antique Czech Art Deco hanging light is truly old, yet it could be the most radical object in the space—a jazz riff visualized in midair.

Opposite and below: An inglenook off of the living room is its own little world, like a dollhouse library spied through a magnifying glass. Unusual Aesthetic Movement armchairs covered in a fabric by Décors Barbares evoke Eastern European associations, while antique Baroque lamps retrofitted with clamshell shades suggest a Latin atmosphere. The figure of the shell, Adam's talismanic sigil, reappears in a hanging light of his own design.

Below: A nineteenth-century majolica stand topped by books serves as a side table. A profusion of antique, vintage, and contemporary objects surround this vignette, yet the total effect is one of serene balance. Adam does not sacrifice clarity for complexity; opulence and editorial rigor are not in opposition.

Opposite: An Aubusson tapestry provides a fanciful backdrop for modular 1970s seating by Klaus Uredat. Such tapestries are a staple of Adam's practice, and they appear in the homes of several other New Antiquarians, transforming urban walls into imaginary landscapes. The hand cushion, Nicola L. eye lamp, and miniature synagogue are typically surreal.

Below: On the dining room table, a sea-floor fantasy by Ficus Interfaith is studded with feasting crabs, oysters, seaweed, starfish, and Adam's initials. In this setting, favrile glass vases take on the appearance of creatures from the ocean deep.

Opposite: Old prints from Matisse's "Jazz" series hang next to a *cartapesta* wall light by F. Taylor Colantonio, which is technically new but feels perfectly ancient. The Lee Dan interphone, a survivor of Old New York, is ancient in a different way—and unplaceably chic.

III

PABLO BRONSTEIN

Deal, England

English silver sugar casters, Chinese export figures, Delft pottery, seventeenth-century candlestands, early Deal memorabilia, and Deal-made objects.

The aesthetic lives of young gay men are easily misunderstood. In the case of Pablo Bronstein, the Argentine-British artist, it has become apocryphal that his grandmother gave him a silver sugar caster at age sixteen, thereby sparking a formative obsession, a lifelong collecting practice, and perhaps even Pablo's career. As a neat little dream of generational inheritance, it's an apocryphon that is difficult to resist.

Of course, almost the reverse is true: after he developed the first stirrings of intensity for the antique silver caster, Pablo convinced his grandmother to yield it to him. Like a magnet, he had drawn the silver caster toward himself—the first of many objects that would pass into his possession, and perhaps his soul, through his own efforts. He had become a collector.

If silver sugar casters didn't exist, Pablo would have invented them. Like so many boys of his disposition, he had a habit of drawing grade-school capriccios: imagined architecture, invariably in the grand manner, that would have been buildable in a more interesting age. In the same year he took possession of the caster, Pablo redecorated his bedroom in "crappy" (his word) Neasden, a northwest London suburb.

I have not seen photos of the room, but it is said to have resembled a Baroque palazzo. Perhaps his grandmother's elegant home in Buenos Aires was an inspiration. I suspect that most of the decor was derived from interior decoration magazines and the young Pablo's fevered imagination.

Like so many boys of his disposition, Pablo proceeded to architecture school, but that is also where his story began to diverge. In a more interesting age, architecture school would have suited him better, and our world would brim with Rococo skyscrapers, brutalist grottos, postmodern follies, and Baroque parking garages designed, with disarming seriousness, by Pablo Bronstein. Pablo is no fool, however, and he quickly understood that his capricious inventions could only be realized, in the real world, as contemporary art. Since then, his work has become even more gloriously unbuildable. The boy from Neasden builds castles in the sky.

Closer to earth, in the sleepy seaside-holiday town of Deal, he builds a collection—and a total environment to contain it. The place was not much to begin with ("an exciting modern Shaker-effect kitchen with pewter-feel handles," read the real estate ad), but that was before it became an unrestrained manifestation of everything an artistic practice cannot be, that a house and collection can. Now it is undoubtedly too much, which is just right.

The hectic "Chinese" room that mercifully replaced that "Shaker-effect kitchen," for instance, looks like nothing more than a ship's cabin designed by Thomas Chippendale—if he were drunk on Chartreuse. There's nothing Chinese about it, and that's the point. The boy from Neasden loves things that are not what they say they are. If that sounds "camp" to you, Susan, it is only to the extent that material culture has always embodied those qualities we narrowly associate, today, with Sontag's famous concept: "artlessly mannered or stylized," "self-consciously artificial and extravagant," "teasingly ingenious and sentimental," to quote the dictionary definition. And indeed, the room's topsy-turvy take on chinoiserie evokes History more fully than any norm-following period room ever could.

It follows that a museum-quality collection of casters figures prominently in the scene. Not that any museum will possess such a collection until Pablo bequeaths his; the grouping, like Pablo's collecting practice, is sui generis. When he began collecting casters serially, he says, he would buy on impulse, struck by the same feelings of intensity that started him down the path to connoisseurship. Squint at a caster long enough and you may begin to see an ornament-encrusted phallus topped by a rather suggestive dome. That is what Pablo sees. When a caster looks just right, it is, in a familiar way, irresistible.

But resist Pablo must, as all of us with expanding collections and shrinking storage must resist, and in recent years he has become scrupulously selective. Will a new acquisition fill a hole in his collection? Will it be as good as or better than the current best example? One day I ask him about this, but my notes are mostly obscured. Instead I see, written out in a clear hand, "Paul de Lamerie—silver centerpiece—spidery, spindly—ultimate acquisition." In other words, the crown jewels for collectors of eighteenth-century silver—not just Rococo, but among the most Rococo things ever made.

If de Lamerie centerpieces didn't exist, I fancy, Pablo would have invented them.

Previous: The fanciful "Chinese" room feels truer to history, somehow, than any period room I've seen in a museum. Once a conventional space, Pablo intervened with Chippendale-inspired fretwork, lashings of arsenic-green paint, chartreuse brocade-upholstered walls, and a dizzying array of antiques reflecting a fever-dream chinoiserie theme. The effect is surprisingly cohesive and cozy, if bracingly unconventional. Across the variegated surfaces of the space, Pablo has inserted his collections—a Regency mirror of papier-mâché, a Spode dessert service from the same period, English and Dutch Delft tiles, even a Japanese theatrical figure in a mask.

Opposite: Across from the fireplace stands a spinet, or miniature harpsichord. Filling the wall above, like visualized sound, are George III wall brackets carved with ho ho (or ho-o) birds. These support a pair of antique porcelain demons of Chinese manufacture. The stage is set for a diabolically entertaining recital, and indeed, the mirror was originally supplied by Oliver Messel, the great English stage designer.

Opposite: In Pablo's world, even bedrooms are like theatrical sets. In this one, thanks to the lampshade, which sports a Venetian scene, the Art Deco headboards recall gondolas. As you drift off to sleep, you may dream of William of Orange's entry to Antwerp—the subject of the engravings above the bed. The pair of Wedgwood plates in the Darwin pattern, a gift from a curator friend, feature an unusual colorway.

Above: An early eighteenth-century Piedmontese chair sits at the ready to hold tomorrow's outfit or support a change of shoes. If you haven't begun collecting yet, start with an antique chair. They are easy to source, sculptural, and practical, and they go anywhere.

Decisively rejecting the white cube approach to making rooms and displaying collections, Pablo dunked his parlor in paint the color of twilight. It serves as a dramatic backdrop for porcelain, but the stars here are a pair of sixteenth- or seventeenth-century marble figures of souls in purgatory—one being Moses, the other an unbaptized infant. Above them, a panel portrait from the same period depicts a gentleman holding an enormous skull. Collecting across periods and disciplines is especially fun when you have a thematic focus, no matter how morbid.

The early eighteenth-century grandfather clock and 1830s police truncheon are local finds from Deal.

Below: Displaying collections can be as much fun as assembling them. Here, a corner cabinet topped by a broken swan's-neck pediment displays Pablo's extensive collection of silver sugar casters, while a drop-front desk holds a colorfully graphic Cantonese chess set carved of ivory—a fixture of haute-bourgeois Latin American interiors like his grandmother's. Like his sugar casters, the chess set casts an invisible thread to the Buenos Aires of Pablo's youth. Watching over the secretly nostalgic scene are a pair of eighteenth-century oak caryatid sirens from a ship. Who knows what they've seen in their long, seafaring lives?

Opposite: A whimsically vertiginous display of ceramics in a corner is steadied, visually, by the symmetrical arrangement of the brackets supporting it. A note of morbidity creeps in through the gruesome Crucifixion scene depicted on the small Leeds creamware pot, upper right. The late eighteenth-century figure of Athena, however, remains breezily unbothered atop her Louis XV bracket. Painted with a delicate chinoiserie scene, the Worcester punch pot once shattered to pieces before being restuck, with loving care, by Pablo.

Opposite: If you ask me, Gentle Reader, good silver and good books are the marks of the good life. Pablo has assembled collections of both in this quiet, Delft-tile-lined corner. At bottom right is a small roundel bearing a watercolor of Voltaire's hearse.

Below: A far cry from the "Shaker-effect" kitchen that came with the house, today's kitchen holds an early seventeenth-century Flemish clothes press; a Regency pearl ware platter printed in the China trade pattern; and a rare, large, and early London Delft charger with large chinoiserie figures, among other precious objects. The lesson is clear: fill your home—even its functional zones—with things you cherish. Even if an object breaks occasionally, it will be worth the sacrifice.

IV

ALEX TIEGHI-WALKER

Echo Park, Los Angeles

Shaker and Shaker-inspired chairs, textiles, mescal cups
and other small drinking vessels, Japanese pottery, and old issues
of *National Geographic* magazine.

Too often we speak of craft as a discrete discipline, like painting or sculpture, instead of giving it the reverence due to a category that encompasses everything made in this world from the dawn of humanity to the age of mechanical production. The first rudimentary tools were examples of craft. So was the Great Pyramid of Giza, along with the entire material world of our ancestors as recently as the nineteenth century.

Alex Tieghi-Walker understands this, and he knows that human beings continue to make much of our world, and undoubtedly the better parts of it, by hand. If you saw him on the street, you might assume that he makes things, too. The beanie installed permanently atop his head conveys the spirit, somehow, of a cheerfully leftist working person, and his sparkly eyes and floor-rattling chuckle recall the mien of a gabby but discreetly wise baker or the mystical kind of furniture-maker who might bellow a profundity amid the hush of a wood-chip-carpeted workshop.

Your assumption would not be altogether wrong. Through his gallery, Tiwa Select, Alex produces permanent environments, temporary installations, and community-minded

happenings that situate the work of self-taught artists—particularly those anchored in tradition-based folk craft practices—with scrupulous care. You might say he is a maker's maker: you make a thing and he will make a space for it in the world. You could even say that he will make a world for it, full stop. He will do so, moreover, with the reverence of one who sees Bronze Age tools and Egyptian pyramids and Belgian lace and Murano glass and Shaker boxes in even the wonkiest hand-thrown mug.

There may be such a mug in your kitchen. Perhaps your wayward best friend threw it in college. Perhaps you did, last week. Or perhaps you picked it up in the Andes, or Japan. No matter its origin or age, if you appreciate that mug, you know what was imbued in its clay at the time of its formation: creativity, humility, patience, and pride in labor well done (or poorly done, but nevertheless completed—a modest victory in itself). If you were to pick up the mug right now, cradle it in your palm, caress it, behold it, and raise it to your lips, you would feel any number of special things. I will pass over those sensations in silence; they are better felt than described. I will only ask this: Can machine-made things evoke such feelings?

Alex knew the joy of the handmade from an early age. The son of an Italian ceramist and a British historian, and the grandson of a quilter and textile collector, he grew up in South Wales, but his mother was a born traveler, and she spirited him away to mainland Europe for budget holidays whenever she could. When he was old enough to spirit himself away, he wandered to Delhi, Mumbai, California, Argentina, and Venice. Everywhere he went, he collected objects. These were not souvenirs, he says; there is no "there" when there is no "here." They were simply passages in an unfolding story.

After a zeitgeisty stint as a journalist and editor in hard-partying Peak London, that story brought him back to Northern California, where he began to unfurl roots. For five happy years he focused on building a community around a winery, a mixed-use farm, and himself, installing—and beginning to sell—his growing collection of craft in a seemingly enchanted redwood barn-house. There, every handmade object, locally sourced dinner, and long conversation contributed to a slower, more intentional life—the hippie-ecological dream of the 1960s realized in our times. When Alex moved to Los Angeles for love, however, and the pandemic rolled around, only the objects remained.

Here, in his former Los Angeles home, Alex can be seen in his element: surrounded by collected textiles, quilts, wall hangings, ceramics, and uncountable chairs that he carries around, from house to house, like a snail's shell. It should come as no surprise that his collection is highly mobile, both within a given room or house and in the broader, and indeed broadest, sense. If you call Alex on a Saturday afternoon, you might find him moving some of those chairs to the edges of his living room to make way for thirty dinner guests.

None of these movements slow him down in any way. Even as he evangelizes the beauty of everyday objects through Tiwa Select, reminding us to slow down and enjoy their tenderness, purity, and soul, he is likely to be charging off on a new personal collecting caper. Sake cups and Delft tiles, for example, are recent obsessions. Once he begins seeing them, they appear everywhere—meaning, all around the globe.

He is sure to seek them out there.

Page 71: In its distressed state, this hanging quilt reveals its age: the newspaper pattern used to piece it together, glimpsed beneath crumbling cotton, dates from the 1920s.

Above: "The best piece of storage I have ever owned," according to Alex, this antique Welsh oak dresser is filled top and bottom with plates, bowls, cups, and glasses collected on his travels. Most of the bowls are Japanese antiques; the cups, of more recent vintage, tend to be Mexican. It is often the case that New Antiquarians are drawn to strange and unusual objects, but common things are increasingly appealing to young collectors—particularly those interested in functional objects produced before the advent of modernism, often in folk craft traditions.

Opposite: On any given Saturday afternoon, you might find Alex moving chairs like this sturdy Windsor to the edges of a room to make way for a crowd of dinner guests. ("Real estate is 'immobilier,'" he might remind you, "but furniture is 'mobilier'!") He is sure to cook a couple of roast chickens for his guests, or a peppery riff on Persian cuisine. Call him the next day and he might tell you he is moving to New York City. The chairs will undoubtedly go with him.

Previous: As you enter the bathroom, you pass beneath a floating shelf made by Robert "Mouseman" Thompson, who worked in Yorkshire at the start of the twentieth century. Mouseman won his moniker by carving a little mouse onto each of his works as a vernacular kind of signature. Close by, a bee box of similar vintage recalls Mouseman's rural world, in which beekeepers would use such a box to monitor the health of a hive. Inside, a shield-back hall chair is stacked with toilet reading, exactly as Alex remembers it in his mother's guest bathroom.

Right: In a multipurpose room that could be given over to eating, meeting, viewing art, or all of these activities at once, another cabinet is full of treasures. Displayed atop it are pots by one of Alex's favorite artists, Andrée Singer Thompson, along with a face jug by Jim McDowell. The compact side chair at rest against the wall came from Shop NFS ("Not For Sale") in Los Angeles; the proprietor, Jonathan Pessin, also a collector, thinks the chair was made in the early 1900s and that the carving on its splat is a masonic symbol. Peer closely at the floor beneath the banged-together table and you will see the remnants of Alex's latest happening. Old things and functional objects, however beautiful, were made to be lived with—which means partied with.

80

Above: Light, sculptural furnishings lend themselves to provisional arrangements that can be easily adjusted for effect, moved around or between rooms, and shipped to new ports of call. Alex's marble-topped Anglo-Indian table has been on the move for generations. Originally belonging to his great-grandparents, who spent most of their lives in India and Sri Lanka, the table descended to Alex through his grandmother. Today, the ornate table lives alongside simple rustic stools and wood slabs. Who knows where it will go next?

V

JEREMY SIMIEN

Baton Rouge, Louisiana

Portraits in oil, Louisiana-made antebellum furniture, portrait miniatures on ivory, Navajo and Pueblo jewelry, cartes de visite, and Southern coin silver.

They say the dead never die, but they are easily forgotten. Sometimes swiftly, sometimes slowly, their things are dispersed, their names go unspoken, and the tide of the living overtakes their memory. The rich, famous, and privileged try to beat back this tide, of course, with records and possessions, while the poor and marginalized are subsumed. The fewer the possessions, the fewer the records, the faster the forgetting.

As Jeremy Simien knows, however, memory can be restored.

A ninth-generation Louisiana Creole of color, he counts the forgotten among his ancestors, who were people of combined European, African, and Native American descent. In the 1830s, at a time when one in ten Black Americans was free, and New Orleans bustled with free people of color, Creoles of color owned a third of the French Quarter. Their homes were filled with luxurious furniture, fine art, and the ephemera of an affluent class. Inside their parlors stood tall armoires and wide secretary desks, and inside these were stashed important documents of all kinds. On the walls were ennobling portraits by Paris-trained artists. Measured in things, the bank of Creole memory was deep.

Unhappily it was not to remain that way. By the mid-nineteenth century, Anglo-American influences had encroached on Louisiana, reinforcing the strict racial binary of Black and White, and a series of apocalypses soon followed: the Civil War, black codes, Reconstruction, Jim Crow laws, and a case of racial and cultural amnesia that persists to this day. Through centuries of migration and struggle, Creole material culture was scattered, destroyed, or disassociated from its context, like the people who once possessed it.

It is possible that none of this would have mattered much to Jeremy, regardless of his ancestry, except he was born curious. Growing up in the 1990s, he preferred fossil-gathering to playing sports, and baseball cards were more interesting to him than the game itself. He read comic books, too, but as intrigued as he was by their stories, he only prized the comics with beautiful covers. On the playground, a combined passion for knowledge and beauty is sure to mark out a boy as unusual, but Jeremy did not see himself as one of life's outcasts. He was and remains a proud rebel, he says, unabashedly following his curiosity wherever it leads. Of course, that is just another way of saying he is a collector, because his curiosity leads him reliably, and you might even say inexorably, toward objects.

When *what* he was caught up with *who* he was, and the idea of collecting Creole material culture struck him, it was as if he had been preparing for the pursuit his whole life. Jeremy's parents had collected antiques they liked the looks of, and he had spent his twenties as a watch connoisseur in training, learning the "good, better, and best" of timepieces from mom-and-pop dealers and the online message boards he frequented, like so many millennials, when the internet still felt like the Wild West. Now nearly thirty, and a full-fledged collector, he began assembling the most important collection of his life: one that would fill the gaps in the history of his family, their people, and himself.

Jeremy's first acquisition was an antique armoire, and he has been tirelessly restoring memory, object by object, since the day he brought it home. His most notable acquisition by a wide margin is a family portrait, commissioned in 1837, depicting three wide-eyed white children and, behind them, a mixed-race teenager of inscrutable mien. The youth's luminous, sympathetically rendered expression demands this exact question: *Who was he?* For a long time, nobody knew, and for an even longer time, he was quite literally missing from the picture, having been painted out of memory in the century following the Civil War, when his presence would have raised uncomfortable questions in a Jim Crow society devoted, with ever-increasing ferocity, to clear racial and social hierarchies.

After years of searching, intensive research with historian Katy Morlas Shannon, and many sleepless nights, the duo was successful in identifying the teenager, or perhaps the teenager was successful in making himself known. When the discovery was announced to the public, Jeremy wrote on Instagram, "Bélizaire, they know your name now. Tell the ancestors to let me sleep for a minute."

I suspect that Jeremy slept for little more than that minute. His web browser is open to an uncountable number of auction sites in seemingly every time zone, and the list of names to uncover is limitless. The dead are easily forgotten, after all, but with enough persistence, they can be remembered.

Page 87: A Parisian woman of color commands your gaze all the way from the turn of the twentieth century. The spare bedroom in which her portrait hangs possesses a broadly Cajun Prairie—or rural Southern Louisiana—character, complete with a salvaged Creole mantel from an ancestor's four-room house built of bousillage, a mixture of clay and Spanish moss. Below the portrait, a vintage tobacco jar jolts visitors with a disquieting reminder of the "mammy" stereotype propagated during the Jim Crow era. Jeremy retains the object as a reminder of that period, and to pay homage to the tignons and madras head wraps worn by women of color throughout Louisiana's history.

Opposite: A visual representation of Creole, this dining room vignette symbolically consigns Napoleon to a tense afterlife with a Chi wara from Mali and the festive trappings of Mardi Gras. By garlanding the emperor with a string of African trade beads, Jeremy—and by extension, his ancestors—enjoy the last laugh against the man who reinstated slavery in France.

Below: Jeremy's collection of portrait miniatures includes rare examples featuring people of color. Based on her fashionable dress, and the mere fact of the miniature's existence, Jeremy guesses that this female sitter in an Empire gown was a free woman of color from Louisiana or the French Caribbean. A redheaded Creole like the one depicted here, in the round frame, may or may not have been (or passed as) white. Among the artists represented in the growing collection are A. D. Lansot, Antonio Meucci, and Ambrose Duval.

91

Previous: In the music room, given over much of the time to reading and research, two Louisiana portraits take pride of place on display easels. While they are nineteenth-century copies, likely by Louis Antoine Collas, the originals were painted by the first Mexican artist of significance in Spanish colonial New Orleans, José Francisco Xavier de Salazar y Mendoza, around 1791–92. Ever intrepid, Jeremy tracked them down in France. Now he can contemplate Mr. and Mrs. Charles Loubies from his eighteenth-century sofa.

Above: Jeremy's five-times great-grandfather was enslaved at birth. In 1841, decked out in finery, George Simien sat for this portrait. After seven years of research, seeking, and finding, Jeremy acquired it from distant cousins in California. Their ancestors having decamped from Louisiana in the 1920s, they were unaware of their own history. Jeremy was not. Thanks to his collecting practice, they now know who they are, and he hosts his many-times grandfather right where he belongs: Louisiana.

Opposite: A Mardi Gras costume hangs above a ladderback chair from the River Parishes, recalling the "country Creole" culture to be found along the banks of the Mississippi River between New Orleans and Baton Rouge.

Below: When you step into Jeremy's house, an Acadian-style new-build on a cul-de-sac in suburban Baton Rouge, you could not be blamed for expecting to find new furniture, little art, and an assortment of flat-screen television sets. Instead, you are confronted by Louisiana history in all its richness. Look one way and the faces of Jeremy's ancestors meet your gaze. Look another and you'll see a nineteenth-century Steinway topped by a fishbowl of pottery sherds unearthed in the Tremé neighborhood of New Orleans. Empire and Louis XV tables are piled high with antique silver and crystal decanters, which are regularly pressed into service. You might even find a tumbler, filled with drink, in your own hand. After being offered a seat, you may land on an eighteenth-century sofa more comfortable than any down-filled sectional available on the market today. Peek inside a drawer in this guest bedroom and you may discover a trove of daguerreotypes, or a sheaf of historic documents awaiting their mounts.

VI

GIANCARLO VALLE & JANE KELTNER DE VALLE

Dumbo, Brooklyn

Midcentury French and Italian design, vintage Elsa Peretti jewelry, children's artwork, contemporary abstraction, and antique tapestries.

Sometimes, in the aisles of antiques fairs, I am accosted by glowering figures of a distinctly unhappy mien. If there are two of them, a man and a woman, and they appear especially dour, I know what they will say before they open their mouths: "Our children don't want our things. We couldn't give away the stuff if we tried!" The stuff and things in question are antiques, of course, and the ungrateful children, I am led to believe, represent all young people everywhere, who universally reject their familial patrimony, thereby disproving any public statements I have made about young collectors.

At these moments I reserve a kind thought for the absent children, fervently hoping, for their sake, that they are roasting on some faraway beach, or getting a new sleeve inked at the tattoo shop, with a modern apartment full of IKEA—or better yet, avant-garde collectible design—to return home to each night. With parents like theirs, who would want family heirlooms?

The case of Giancarlo Valle and Jane Keltner de Valle is the exact opposite. The children of collectors, they continue the tradition of connoisseurship in a breezy but thoughtful way that speaks well of their parents and bodes well for the

future of collecting in their own young family. Indeed, if any children are susceptible to the collecting bug, it will be Giancarlo and Jane's. They stand to inherit excellent examples of twentieth-century design, among other choice objects, but the inheritance of property cannot be the soul of collecting in the twenty-first century. We live too long for that now. Instead, it is an attitude toward things, more than anything, that we can bequeath to the next generation.

Ask yourself: *If I were a small child, would I enjoy the way my family lives with old things?* If the answer is no, either loosen up instantly or prepare to accost me at the Park Avenue Armory in a couple of decades. When you walk into Giancarlo and Jane's apartment in Brooklyn and imagine how their children might respond, the answer is an emphatic yes. The kids enjoy it here.

Because Giancarlo is a talented architect, the ease of the place emanates, to some extent, from its bones. The building's concrete-block skeleton has been left intact but delicately reskinned with plaster, veiled in canopies, and colorfully striped. The result is a sort of jungle gym in the sky, if an unusually elegant and cerebral one.

In the living area, beneath a massive bank of windows, Giancarlo has run a playful panel of ondulation right across the space so that the room, and the big New York City view, seem to float above an ancient sea. A favorite of midcentury French designer Jean Royère, the wave motif went viral in the design world around the start of the pandemic, but this room was designed before all of that, and happily, Giancarlo has a *longue-durée* view of design. The wave is a timeless symbol, he says, familiar from myriad cultures. It grounds the apartment in a deep, unplaceable feeling of play—and history.

Antiques and vintage material fulfill a similar function: the decoration of each room spins around objects from Giancarlo and Jane's collection. A salmon-hued marble coffee table designed by Gae Aulenti, for example, serves as the indestructible centerpiece of the playroom. The couple repeats like a mantra that design is meant to be lived with and enjoyed, which perhaps means jumped upon. Still, they do not buy with an eye toward indestructibility. "Sometimes people with children think you can't invest in anything nice because they'll destroy it," said Jane to me one day while the children ate lunch in the kitchen. "But when you're looking at vintage pieces, they've already been around for decades. They've already dealt with children!" Added Giancarlo, deadpan, from the next room: "They've already been destroyed."

Jane, a former style director at *Architectural Digest*, and the founder of a children's skincare line, grew up in a Keith Irvine–decorated apartment across the river in Manhattan. She learned from a young age that you could live comfortably with old things, and her parents only collected what they liked—objects that felt true to their taste. They themselves had a good example to follow: Jane's grandfather had been a collector and patron of Native American art, and the entry hall Jane passed through every day, growing up, was filled with material inherited from him.

Today, in addition to the things you see in these pages, Jane collects vintage jewelry designed by Elsa Peretti, and as we talk, I realize that the collecting categories she explores will only proliferate with the years. Her curiosity is her true inheritance.

It will also, I suspect, be the children's.

Page 101: In Giancarlo and Jane's kitchen, an unexpected pair of alabaster urns and a vintage tole basket are in active use. The urns were bought at auction in Litchfield, Connecticut, an antiques epicenter not far (but many worlds away) from Brooklyn.

Previous: A wall-mounted mobile lamp, designed by Giancarlo in collaboration with Ladies & Gentlemen Studio, sets a ludic tone in the kid-friendly dining area. The dynamic diptych is by Christopher Astley, and collected vessels include a vintage terra-cotta carafe and pitcher by Elsa Peretti for Tiffany and a playful, blossom-dotted vase by Jordan McDonald. You will find no fragile glass here. You will also find no loot. The V-leg chairs are contemporary reeditions of one of Pierre Jeanneret's iconic designs for the planned administrative city of Chandigarh, hand-crafted, like the originals, by Indian artisans. These are an ethical alternative to vintage examples removed from the city by Western dealers, robbing Chandigarh of its material heritage.

Right: Giancarlo's father traveled regularly to Uganda and Ethiopia during his childhood, always bringing home a wooden mask, a carved bowl, or a textile. Later, living in Caracas and Guatemala City, the Valles acquired more examples of local craft, in addition to heirlooms inherited from their Italian-Peruvian family in South America. The Ethiopian chief chair by the windows reflects this family collecting tradition and inspired, in the foreground, Giancarlo's beloved Smile chair. A vintage coffee table by Milo Baughman anchors the room. Beside the sofa is a 1950s French butcher-block table; above it is a contemporary work by Jayson Musson. A pair of lounge chairs by Gio Ponti peek out from the lower left corner. Above them, just outside the frame, is an Aubusson tapestry from the 1760s.

Opposite: In the passage to the family's bedrooms, a carved wooden children's chair from the 1920s offers little ones a place to pull on shoes. An artwork by one of the couple's children shines forth from a vintage frame.

Above: Contrasting the ondulating panel in the study is a faceted wood-and-plastic lamp designed by Rudolf Steiner for Dörfler Dornach in the 1960s. Nearby is a stool by Green River Project. Leaning against the bookshelves, a photograph of Yves Saint Laurent's office by Gilles Bensimon reveals a key influence. So do the volumes in the couple's design reference library, which spans centuries and continents.

VII

JARED FRANK

Silver Lake, Los Angeles

Oddfellows folk art, trompe l'oeil furniture, vintage textiles, gilded mirrors, oversized playing card memorabilia, masks, and family heirlooms.

If you shut your eyes and conjure a capital-*C* Collection, you might dredge up an image of a long gallery lined with paintings and sculptures, shelves sagging beneath the weight of old china, or a climate-controlled closet containing what we have come to call, with a degree of self-importance, archival fashion. Libraries, humidors, or wine cellars might float through your vision. So too might a dining table laid thick with precious silver. To understand Jared Frank, you have to forget all of that.

Although he is a connoisseur in the making, Jared is not a serial collector, and the norms of taxonomic collecting interest him little. While he appreciates originality, fine craftsmanship, and the nuances of condition, these factors do not motivate his collecting practice. Neither does elite provenance, the latest entrant in the pantheon of connoisseurial considerations. Stepping inside Jared's lair at Casa Larissa, a Los Angeles apartment building finished about two minutes before the Wall Street Crash of 1929, you must also forget about the earlier *Wunderkammer* tradition of collecting. Jared's apartment looks like a "cabinet of curiosities," but it is no mere showcase for the curiosities it contains.

Indeed, the apartment itself is the most important item in Jared's collection. The objects are supporting players.

Take one glance at the trompe l'oeil murals and exuberant floor paintings that decorate the rental and you will see why. They aren't decorations for a jewel box; they are the jewels. The fuming censers, cherry-eating birds of paradise, and feats of imaginary architecture were left behind by the unit's previous tenant, Lance Gaylord Klemm, a local painter forced by illness to vacate his Gesamtkunstwerk. When Jared visited the apartment for a sale of Klemm's possessions, he felt that rare thing: a thrilling conviction that he had encountered something wholly original. Happily it was felt too by a sympathetic landlord who wished to keep the place intact. In a world addicted to white paint, the beauty of personality prevailed. Jared moved in on the last day of Klemm's lease.

Since then, he has dedicated himself to assembling a collection based not on his personal preoccupations, which skew toward modernism, but on the needs of the total environment he stewards. A designer by trade, Jared favors the context of place over the more abstract allure of art and objects selected on their own merits. If an object evokes a sense of magic, wonder, alchemy, or enchantment, he says, it could be a good fit for Casa Larissa, regardless of its quality, condition, or even his own feelings about the thing. He is not building a museum-quality collection, after all, but a sort of house museum: one devoted to Klemm's vision, and also to Casa Larissa herself.

The building makes her own demands. A Spanish Revival dream on the cusp of becoming a night terror, the jasmine-embanked building is suspended figuratively, if not quite literally, between *Sunset Boulevard* and *Mulholland Drive*. If rumors are to be believed, the complex once sheltered washed-up Silent Era homosexuals, Rock Hudson's boy toys, and James Dean, or seemingly anyone at the center of the Venn diagram dedicated to "lost souls" and "sexual deviants." Later on, according to legend, the Rolling Stones' mistresses were moved in for a spell. On a sunny day, of course, bardo looks like bohemia. In the 1980s and '90s, the building played host to all-night drag parties and, if whispers are to be believed, a "dungeon." The fun kind.

To honor the genii locorum, Jared moves through the place like a modern-day Renzo Mongiardino, rigging up his finds from the Long Beach Antique Market as if he's designing a stage set. Depending on which way you look, you might find yourself in a Busby Berkeley musical, a Baroque palace, or a broken carnival ride. Like Hollywood itself, the apartment wants to be (or at least look like) all of these things at once.

Often it succeeds in the illusion. By day, a game of pachinko on the living room wall appears to be an intriguing example of folk art. By night, however, you realize that Jared has placed a series of red bulbs where the balls would be, were the game in active use. When he hosts performances and happenings in the room, the bulbs light right up, transforming the board game into a dazzling little proscenium.

In these moments, the apartment really is a stage set, and Jared's friends put on shows that could only happen on this side of bardo—where the trompe l'oeil is realer than real, static objects come magically to life, and absolutely anything could happen, then fade into the walls.

Opposite: Jared is taken with the more curious aspects of our natural and unnatural world, and Casa Larissa brims with references to magic, games, the hermetic, and the occult. Sometimes you do not notice; sometimes you do. Here, punctuating the ziggurat-like mantel designed by the apartment's former tenant, Lance Gaylord Klemm, you may notice a set of cast-iron shooting gallery targets resembling a playing-card suite. These were produced by William F. Mangels, "the Wizard of Eighth Street," a manufacturer of amusement best known for his work on Coney Island. Look closely at the objects surrounding the targets: they provide a master class in composition. First there is collecting, then there is displaying!

Above: At Casa Larissa, objects and architecture are in constant dialogue—or perhaps they are engaged in a dance. Here, the Italian faux-parchment table by Aldo Tura recalls the trompe l'oeil frescoes throughout the apartment and looks as if it has emerged, suddenly in three dimensions, from the painted floor.

115

Opposite and above: A decade into Jared's time at Casa Larissa, his landlord opened a storage closet to reveal a trove of art abandoned by former tenants. Among the hokey canvases was a collection of handmade masks designed not to be worn but displayed like relics from an ancient land. It is somehow unsurprising that, upon expressing admiration for the masks, Jared was informed that they had belonged to his predecessor in the apartment, Klemm, who had collected them from a hairdresser-slash-artist friend—another magical coincidence in a string of them. Since then, the masks have been restored to their rightful home. Beelzebub presides over the entrance to Jared's bedroom.

Opposite: In the kitchen hangs a TWA poster advertising tourism in the Holy Land that was designed by David Klein and salvaged from the travel agency owned by Jared's grandmother. Photographs of family and "instant relatives," as well as mysterious strangers, recur throughout the apartment. On the side of family, his grandmother and great-aunt are pictured here singing for war bonds. On the side of instant relatives are a Roma family surrounded by a hand-painted mat board and a young man who decorated his own mat with prestigious emblems evoking his goals in life. On the side of mysterious strangers, framed photos depict the rites of the Shriners fraternal organization, and a magician posing with his trained fox. Completing the display are rows of tiny smelting pots, painters' palettes, and vintage dolls inspired by *Alice's Adventures in Wonderland*.

VIII

CAMILLE OKHIO

Boerum Hill, Brooklyn

Early Americana, antique textile fragments, brass and iron candlesticks,
Venetian glass miniatures, radical twentieth-century design,
contemporary paintings, and books.

If time travel is possible, Camille Okhio is almost certainly a time traveler. Whether she hails from the future or the past, however, will likely remain a mystery: she seems to belong, like a sort of Time Lord, to all eras. Just when you've pegged her as a thong-bikini-wearing modern, she appears in the *New York Times*—or, if you're lucky, in your life—bedecked in an antique Greek fustanella or a vast, flower-sprigged bonnet. And those are just her clothes. Her household possessions, too, refuse to follow the clock, slipping between periods as easily as Camille changes outfits, and centuries.

Her taste for timelessness—or timefulness—is a sign of the zeitgeist identifiable throughout this book, but Camille is no follower. A design editor by trade, she plays Pied Piper for a generation of nascent collectors who prize authenticity, craftsmanship, and a quality of surprise in the objects they collect (and, critically, use in daily life), ushering in what she terms a "craft renaissance." Handwork and demonstrations of skill catch her eye, but so do virtuoso displays of design ingenuity, artistic expression, and the novel effects of time and chance on objects. In her world, "antique" is a good word, and it is even a little edgy. Through her savvy

recontextualization of tradition (think: bonnets and thongs), the past becomes edgier still—bleeding into the contemporary until it's impossible to tell what is when.

In her compact apartment, a swirling, metallic chair of mysterious origins sits between a puddled curtain and a glowing fragment of stained glass, each object echoing, clarifying, and intensifying the others. While the composition is beautiful, beauty is not its purpose, but a discovery to be made after close looking. As you focus your gaze, seeing past the formal qualities of the scene, you may begin to wonder: *Where are these things from? When are they from?* A sudden richness may fill the air as you realize it is impossible to say.

The Time Lord has achieved her end.

What decoration there is, around the edges, evokes the work of Axel Vervoordt shot through with suggestions of Americana and Afrofuturism, like a Belgian monastery reconstituted in a Pennsylvania barn and airlifted to Lagos (in the year 2347). For every New Antiquarian decorating with ribald color and layer upon layer of pattern, there is a New Antiquarian of a minimalist bent: millennial and Gen Z John Pawsons, almost priestly in their precision, but holding to a more capacious concept of minimalism than their forebears. Camille is one of these. Without sacrificing rigor in the background, her voracious sensibility allows a heedless range of forms, colors, and cultural influences to come to the fore. The spirit of restraint persists, but it is relative now: a pliable medium that sets off moments of abandon rather than an absolute end in itself. (Moreover, in a digital age of ultimate plurality, when every image is indexed, modernist-minimalism is not the only—or even the primary—reference point for restraint. Camille's minimalism is as likely to draw upon refined Ngil masks, spare seventeenth-century ironwork, or elegant Shaker basketry as the International Style.)

And restraint, after all, has its limits. After Camille has deployed it to her ends, there may follow an explosion of vermiculation, a riot of unexpected color, or the deepest, freest laugh you have ever heard.

As she said to me recently, emitting one of those laughs, "I like to create problems for myself, in my home and collection, and then solve them." The solution could take the form of a new acquisition, the deaccessioning of an object that no longer belongs, a splash of red on a white wall, or a fresh arrangement of things that dispels preconceived notions about how objects should be displayed together.

A young visionary who has established herself equally in history and the present, Camille shuttles between both halves of the hourglass as if the gravity of time did not exist. It does, of course, but she vanquishes it by ignoring old ideas about what feels new. We can only hope she retains her temporal powers, because in Camille's interiors, as in her writing, material culture is always interesting, and it always matters intensely: always has, always will.

Opposite: Apartment living in New York City demands space efficiency. When folded up, this midcentury table serves as a display for a vintage Greek souvenir vase and a nineteenth-century miner's lunch box found at an antiques shop in Maine. Extended, it becomes a setting for convivial dinner parties. A vintage obi and a coated plush star by designer Isabella Norris prompt hushed (or raucous) conversation.

Above: A contemporary-Baroque glass by Valentina Cameranesi Sgroi, inspired by marine creatures and the production design of fantasy film *Labyrinth* (1986), sits comfortably next to a glass sardine from Murano. Few would expect to find such objects arranged on a nineteenth-century American step-back cupboard, yet the simple vignette feels as natural and inevitable as the wear on the cupboard's old surface.

Opposite: A fragment of an antique embroidered panel hangs above a modern daybed. By day, this tableau is a clever study in vermiculation. In candlelight, the wavy lines shimmer and dance. Close to the ceiling, a work by artist and designer Susan Cianciolo initiates a dialogue between textiles past and present.

Above: Visual rhymes appear in every corner of Camille's apartment. Here, a puddled curtain echoes the swirling lines of a postmodern bent plywood side chair and a fragment of nineteenth-century Italian stained glass. A ceramic moon jar by Ramsay Kolber hangs above the room.

Like the drop leaf table nearby, Camille's cheerfully demotic vintage secretary desk is a workhorse. Inside it are all the accoutrements of a devoted twenty-first-century epistler. When the desk is closed, your attention is drawn from antique pens and wax seals to a thrifted aluminum vase, an eighteenth-century French rushlight, and a contemporary urushi lacquer bowl showing the many steps of the lacquering process. Above them hangs a daily reminder to "Hold Fast."

IX

COLLIER CALANDRUCCIO

Crown Heights, Brooklyn

Sixteenth- to eighteenth-century tapestries, parcel-gilt furniture,
ancient Greek and Roman objects, Alpine landscapes,
and klismos chairs.

We make a mistake if we think that collecting is related, even remotely, to hoarding. Hoarders have their rights, to be sure, and I should very much like to read a book on the New Hoarders, who are undoubtedly a jolly group. Whereas their practice is centripetal, however, always closing in on itself (and the rooms that contain it), the practice of a connoisseur-collector is more likely to be centrifugal in its force and effect, spinning out into the world in a thousand magnificent ways.

Probably Collier Calandruccio has referred to himself as a hoarder, with adorable self-effacement, at a cocktail party. If he did so, it would have been to charming effect, but he would have been wrong. Indeed, Collier, even more than a collector, is the opposite of a hoarder: he is an antiques dealer. In this role, his job is not to retain objects but to release them into the world—and to his clients. The treasures he brings to light spin right out of his arms and into theirs.

Financial considerations alone do not transform a New Antiquarian into a jobbing dealer. Stocks and bonds buy far more furniture than furniture does, and many dealers enjoy economic security from a young age. So why would

a connoisseur-collector choose a life of spinning and set up shop? And why would Collier, in particular, set up shop—as Klismos Gallery—in his Brooklyn apartment?

We might also ask ourselves, *Why would a fox move into a hen house?* We can only presume it would be pleasant to live with one's quarry.

For Collier, dealing from home offers a chance to be surrounded, day and night, by the objects of his affection: parcel-gilt pier tables, silk lambrequins, Meiji vases, Alpine landscapes, and, of course, klismos chairs. To him, these are not just fine things but entire cosmos unto themselves, each one warranting the closest attention, care, and scholarly study. A deep path has been cut between Collier's dreams, his apartment, and Room 300 at the New York Public Library.

Collier's connoisseurial training, like his dreams, began at a young age. As a boy, he beachcombed along the Gulf Coast, learning to distinguish fossilized shark teeth from the lighter smithereens of seashells tumbled in by the surf. Later, he visited distant relations in old family homes in Mississippi and Virginia, inspecting heirloom furniture, works of art, and mementos accumulated over the centuries. In those living, breathing troves of artifacts he learned how to *look*, and he learned the names of things.

He learned, too, about how to live with the past. "My mother," he once told me, "saved sections of an enormous, unusable family rug—a nineteenth-century Persian Mahal—and faced down-filled pillows with it." Growing up, these were always at his back.

For an eighth-grade history project, he even carved a model of a lost family home, Dungeness, which burned to the ground in 1866. Built of tabby, with a green copper roof, the Federal mansion had been a landmark to sailors navigating the waters around Cumberland Island, Georgia. Now, in the early 2000s, it was known only through a handful of descriptions and cartes de visite of its picturesque ruins. Collier reconstituted the architecture with the aid of pattern books by Asher Benjamin and Palladio's *Four Books of Architecture*. Today, the inveterate classicist could give you an accurate account of what the house's contents might have been.

Given such a wide exposure, such a fertile practice, and the ability to continue broadening it, you might suspect that Collier is reluctant to close the canon and land on a final, static expression of his taste. Why start the clock on finished rooms when you could float in an endless orbit of wonder and discovery, changing up your rooms whenever you like? And what would permanence look like, anyway, for that most centrifugal of collectors: the dealer?

Only a fool would think it looks like things.

Instead, watching Collier light up because an eighteenth-century secretary is leaving his possession, I realize it is the practice of dealing itself that is permanent. Antiques dealers are the opposite of hoarders, after all, and Collier is on a mission to fill the world, not just his own apartment, with a beauty beyond possession.

Above: A desultory cliché of recent times is that antiques should be mixed with modern and contemporary things in order to seem relevant. Collier roundly rejects this premise. Here, Italian giltwood sconces emerge from a sixteenth-century Flemish tapestry depicting Queen Esther, setting off a Florentine portrait of a lady (lowercase *p*, lowercase *l*). A rare Louis XIII settee is covered in late seventeenth-century *cuir de Cordoue*. No live-edge table is needed to bring the scene to life.

Opposite: A bronze portrait bust of a child by Nicolas-Victor Vilain sits on a rosewood William IV pedestal covered in Prelle silk. Perennially unloved and undervalued, William IV furniture (1830–1837) has been described by scholar Andrew Sanders as "Regency putting on weight." A neglected middle child of the English decorative arts, it was swiftly followed by the attention-grabbing (some might say "attention-seeking") productions of the Victorian era.

Collier's apartment is an Aladdin's den of important antiques, but he lives with these masterpieces of design in great comfort. Neutral-hued walls are by turns rich or serene and ward off any stuffiness. They also allow the Oushak rug and galloping parcel-gilt chairs to (quite literally, in the case of the chairs) shine. Produced by Gillows of Lancaster around 1806, the chairs are identical to a set supplied to the Earl of Eglinton at Coilsfield, one of the great lost Regency houses of Scotland—light-years away from twenty-first-century Brooklyn. To the left of the room is a Tuscan *scrittoio* from the dawn of the seventeenth century. It supports a bronze relief once owned by the Canessa brothers, a trio of Italian antiquarians or smugglers, depending on whom you ask, who were active in Naples, Paris, and New York from the late nineteenth century through the 1920s. On the chimney breast, a gentleman depicted in an 1840s portrait seems to contemplate the scene.

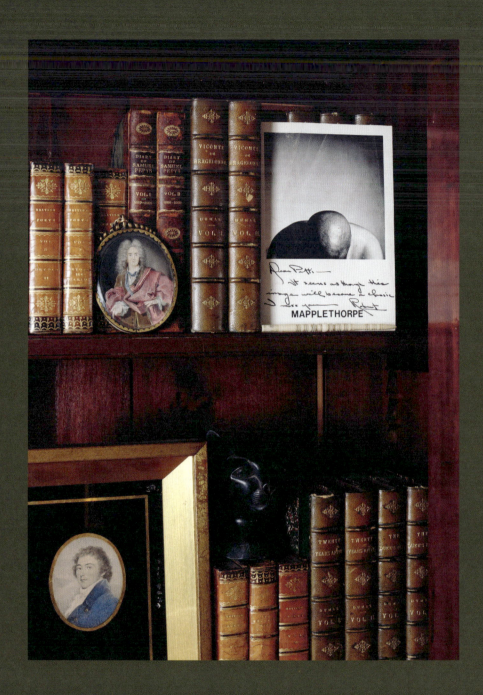

Above: Inside a Grecian Plain style secretary attributed to Duncan Phyfe are inherited portrait miniatures, a rare complete set of *British Poets*, and a 1978 gallery invitation inscribed by Robert Mapplethorpe for Patti Smith. Collier found the delicious piece of ephemera in a chest of drawers not far from the Clinton Hill townhouse where Mapplethorpe and Smith lived as young bohemians in the late sixties.

X

KYLE MARSHALL

Locust Valley, New York

Moonlit seascapes, Outer Lands townies in art, portraits,
American and painted furniture, textiles, and books and pamphlets.

Kyle Marshall might have washed up from the sea. As you follow him around his early nineteenth-century homestead in the hamlet of Locust Valley, near the Long Island Sound, you half expect for salt and sand to shake out of his trouser legs. Then he tells you about his coastal childhood, passed a few miles away, and his briny, windswept mien is explained. More water nymph than child, he grew up submerged in the Sound, and he has returned to this island to be submerged once again in the environment of his youth.

Perhaps "submerged" is not quite the right word, since he has a vessel now: the farmhouse, which lies directly in the path of the town cannon—a make-do veterans memorial of the sort you frequently see but never give a thought to. If the German 77 were to go off, it would blow straight through the house, brush the tops of Kyle's backyard hydrangeas, and land in his hayloft barn-cum-home gym, where I suspect he would use the cannonball as a weight. Certainly he would not be alarmed: Long Island farmhouses are hardy and ever-changing, as he explains in his 2019 book about them, *Americana: Farmhouses and Manors of Long Island*. Long Island collections, too.

(Indeed, in these parts, an old house is the first and last object of—and practically a prerequisite for—any great collection.)

A trained architect, working now as a creative director for an interiors brand, Kyle could easily employ a more conventional approach, gut-renovating the house, installing climate control, and quickly filling the refrigerated space with deracinated collections in a clamor of auction wins and buying trips. Instead, he is following in local tradition and allowing the objects he loves to accrete, just as homesteads do, over time. The vessel is in motion; ballast will be added at successive ports of call.

The carved New Hampshire bedstead in his guest room is a particularly notable piece of ballast, not least because it is put to frequent use by Kyle's roundabout of house guests. (A great many antique beds, being shorter than contemporary models, sit unused in sad warehouses.) When a dealer friend called to offer up a spare canopy bed, Kyle reported that he had just won a tester at auction in a "small bidding war." Still in the glow of victory, Kyle was surprised to learn that his friend had been the underbidder. "I would have kept bidding you up," said his unknowing opponent, "but I had to take a phone call!" (Such are the contingencies in the lives of collectors.) And while Kyle's own bed is a makeshift affair, I suspect a glorious antique will wash in with the tide one day soon and never float away.

Downstairs, between bookcases stacked with Mitfordania and an antique secretary given over, as its maker intended, to epistolary paraphernalia, Kyle entertains. Taken by the romance of grand but threadbare English country-house living, the natural counterpart of Yankee frugality, he serves potato chips in good silver bowls and Orange Crush in good crystal, and he amuses all comers with a wry, literary wit that shimmers, like his collection, between Anglo and American modes.

Glance around and your eye is sure to alight on a sturdy example of Americana, or an arrangement of potatoes where the flowers should be, before flicking to a classical bust and expanses of well-worn English chintz. If you've had a martini or two (bone dry, up, with a twist), as the evening sets in, rocking to and fro, you may begin to feel you're on a ship that plies the Atlantic ports.

So natural and unaffected is the mix that, with a third martini, you might even imagine Kyle as a towheaded youngster swimming out beyond the Sound to England itself. Somewhere in the Sargasso Sea he passes Katharine Hepburn taking her icy morning constitutional, and the two exchange lockjaw greetings between breast strokes, the boy en route to Stowe House and Knole and inspiration across the ocean.

Perhaps that's taking fancy rather too far, you may say, but the atmosphere invites it. Kyle's is an Atlantic life, and his collection floats effortlessly between shores: the near and the far, the mundane and the magical, somehow never very far apart.

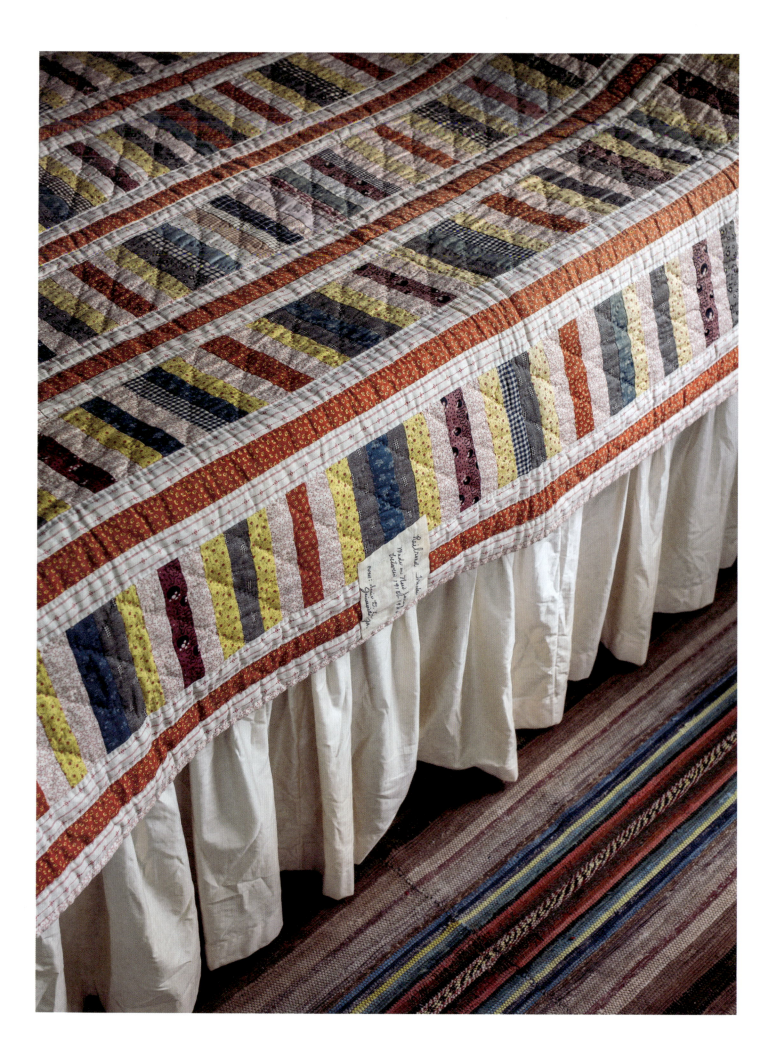

Opposite: Graphic American textiles strike up a conversation in the guest bedroom. The rag carpet was found in Maine. On the quilt is a handwritten label specifying its pattern (Railroad Tracks) and the details of its production ("Made in New Jersey between 1915–1920"). When shared hospitably with friends, as here, a personal collection can bring joy to many.

Above: When Kyle says he "found" something, he really means it. In the front parlor sits a chintz-covered armchair found in a barn on Centre Island, a peninsular village nearby. Possibly he floated it home. The mantel holds an Art Nouveau candlestick and a jug sourced by Calvin Churchman, a designer, like Kyle, with an eye for good things. A Romanian kilim is a footstep-muffling reminder of the Old World across the sea.

Opposite: Among Kyle's many collections is one of English and American candlesticks, only part of which is seen here. When collections like this are ready to hand, you will never be in want of a centerpiece. Just add potatoes, and a houseplant! Danish Deco chairs in the style of Axel Einar Hjorth surround the dining table. These bear evocative carvings of scenes from nature, each one set off by a scalloped frame.

Above: An altar to beauty can be practical, too. In the dining room, a Victorian chest of drawers with an old, teal-painted surface serves as a staging area for meals. Off-duty, it holds hotel silver bowls filled variously with matches and potato chips, a candle snuffer from Kyle's aunt, and a supply of Laura Bagnato–designed napkins from Tiwa Select, the gallery of another New Antiquarian, Alex Tieghi-Walker. A Paul Jasmin collotype of a nude sunbather presides over the scene.

XI

SEAN MCNANNEY & SINAN TUNCAY

Williamsburg, Brooklyn

Ceramics of various periods, textiles from around the world, glass, decorated boxes, antique books, Ottoman miniature paintings on manuscripts, and clothing.

For all the talk of New York City becoming a playground for the rich, there is, in the year 2023, a type of inhabitation—closely related to the treehouse—that remains relatively accessible to the impecunious, unconventional, and adventuresome. These are called walk-up apartments, and until the last one is razed, eccentrics with the thighs of mountaineers are sure to call the city home.

    Sean McNanney and Sinan Tuncay are two of these mountaineers, and beyond lugging themselves and their groceries up and down the heights of their building, they haul an inordinate number of artworks, objects, and (there is no other word for it) curiosities up and into their top-floor railroad apartment, from which these things may never descend. The photos in these pages are tacit proof of the couple's physical fitness, and they reveal their considerable talent as orchestrators of what we might call the theater of life. This theater, as New Yorkers know, can play out behind any door, up any staircase, within any apartment—or treehouse. In Sean and Sinan's, it plays out in an enfilade of rooms given over to the making of new things (Sean is a designer, Sinan an artist), the collecting of old things, and the

practice of living beautifully and thoughtfully in their midst.

Impecunious? No. Unconventional and adventuresome? Read on.

For when you step through Sean and Sinan's front door, you are in a tenement kitchen, and if you look down, or into a mirror, you might expect to find yourself dressed in 1890s garb. Or perhaps the 1890s are dressed in *you*. The ochrey-umbery plaster peels in a way that feels distinctly pre–moon landing, and while the papier-mâché bread trays, Uzbek bowls, and Aesthetic Movement plates are very fine, they have the look of cargo carried over the sea in a great jumble, along with Jack Dawson, below the waterline. Maggie (*A Girl of the Streets*) would feel right at home. It is doubtful, however, that she would have possessed a punk rock portrait roundel, an ironic wristwatch wall clock, or a framed cover of *Queer Stories About Queer Animals*. If she had, I'm guessing they would have had a less ironic valence: more magpie, less gay liberation.

Taking in these anachronisms, you could be forgiven for asking, *When am I?*

As you step into the next room, you are shuttled right out of Tenement City into a more opulent world of Ottoman associations. You may be in the 2020s now, but you are not in Brooklyn. From a position high above the room, in the center of a symmetrical salon-style hang, a beturbaned man presides over the scene, which consists of a divan, of sorts, and a low bookcase topped by objets and mementos. Most of these are Turkish, like Sinan, but there are European things—and even a painting by Sean's mother—mixed in here and there. Like Turkey, and Sinan, this little lounge in the center of the apartment syncretically straddles spheres.

The next room in the enfilade is the couple's bedroom, which evokes Venice and Egypt as much as Turkey. Pausing for a moment in yet another slippery, sphere-straddling room, you could be forgiven for asking, *Where am I?*

The answer becomes clear when you reach, in the next, inordinately yellow room, the terminus of the apartment. Here, the material culture of seemingly every time and place is on display, and any question of when or where you are flies out of the window. (And there *are* windows here, at the back of the walk-up.) A flock of Chinese ceramic parrots, collected individually over time, hovers near the ceiling. Behind them is an 1840s Italian mirror hanging against a frieze drawn by Sean in the faintest, most elegant hand. A Biedermeier armchair beckons you to sit and admire it all. Inevitably, however, your eye will be drawn to the collection of homoerotic art covering every wall and surface of the room except for the floor. It would take a small team of art historians and archaeologists to count all of the buttocks, and at no point in the process would they wonder when or where they are. Neither would you.

For here, at the heart of Sean and Sinan's collection, in the theater of their life, you could be nowhere else. Only a walk-up apartment on a quiet street in Williamsburg could hold so much of the world. Only up an endless staircase, your legs aching, could you open a door on quite so many times and places (and buttocks).

New York City may be a playground for the rich, but for now, at least, it remains a playground for the rich in imagination, too. If you know where to look, and you have strong thighs, you can climb the stairs and find it.

Opposite and below: Many years of collecting produced the apparently effortless potpourri on display in Sean and Sinan's sitting room. Amid the ode to the male form are romantic objects selected for their own, non-figural qualities: a sconce designed by Christopher Dresser, a Biedermeier armchair, an Aesthetic Movement lamp, and Ottoman hookah bases. Extending the erotic lounge atmosphere are pillows covered in a variety of materials, from Mongolian silk velvet to Wiener Werkstätte lace. An embroidered silk specimen is from Sinan's great-grandmother.

Overleaf: While Sean and Sinan collect widely, with the construction of a total world in mind, they also maintain deep, serial collections of objects such as these Chinese ceramic parrots, which have been in continuous production since the eighteenth century. Like other discerning collectors, they tend to avoid examples produced after the Second World War.

Opposite and above: New Antiquarians tend to populate their kitchens and bathrooms with objects from their collections, and Sean and Sinan are no exception. You only live once, their kitchen implies, so enjoy your things while you can. Papier-mâché bread trays, antique photographs, framed book covers, and a 1990s charcoal portrait of Sean decorate the space, along with uncountable other items. Collected bowls from Uzbekistan and an eighteenth-century Italian painted chair are in active use. The reader should note that the pair of straw slippers by Stubbs & Wootton were not styled. When you live with beautiful things, whether they are new or old, happenstance conspires to produce picturesque results.

XII

ABEL SLOANE & RUBY WOODHOUSE

Clapton, London

Lace samples, fabrics and textiles, ceramics, cardboard furniture, Watcombe terra-cotta jugs, design ephemera, and things made by friends.

Old Master paintings were contemporary once, and antiques were not antique at the time of their creation. They were new, of course, and sometimes radically so. Long before the advent of modernism, it was not unusual for one style to supplant another in a violent rejection of what came before. Indeed, some of today's antiques began life, ironically, as examples of an avant-garde set firmly against the past. Put differently: Grandma might have been a punk in her youth.

Our ideas about old things—and elderly people—rarely accommodate such possibilities, focusing instead on the sheer fact of age. As any Jane Fonda or Diane Keaton comedy of the past decade will tell you, however, this is a mistake. Many of life's survivors remain permanently young at heart. And while objects, like humans, do age, becoming materially different over time, their dings, pitting, patina, and craquelure, like wrinkles, indicate only that they have led full lives.

The radicalism of old things should become more evident as the material culture of modernism enters the Valhalla of the antique. The Bauhaus was founded in 1919, after all; its earliest products are already, as of 2019, antiques. Each successive year brings a wave of new entrants to the canon.

Established design icons are just the start. Greater age reliably yields greater value in the antiques market, and as "vintage" material becomes "antique," the economic incentive for dredging up overlooked examples of modern design will only increase. Businesspeople disguised as specialists will seek to capitalize on this opportunity. Like mercenaries fighting in a strange land, however, their hearts will not be in the task. Neither will their eyes. On the hunt for new finds, they are likely to miss what is in front of them. Collectors motivated by passionate curiosity, such as Abel Sloane and Ruby Woodhouse, will not. More like priests than mercenaries, their calling is to reveal what has been forgotten. Those with eyes to see will benefit greatly from paying attention.

The son of a London cab driver, Abel was an English major doing restoration work on the side when he began collecting. After a few lucky finds, he entered the trade, naming his business after the year, 1934, when Gerrit Rietveld designed his crate furniture series. The tone was set. At first, he focused on furniture sourcing and restoration. When he was joined by Ruby, a graphic designer and photographer, 1934 expanded to encompass interior design, creative consulting, styling, and storytelling.

The pair soon authored a book, *The Simple Heart of Plywood*, about Makers of Simple Furniture, an interwar English design firm devoted to making modern furniture accessible to all. Founded by a husband-wife duo, Gerald Summers and Marjorie Butcher, the firm is known for bent plywood designs that were "shaped for purpose," to quote a 1933 poem by Summers, with unwavering functionalist scruples that would make Alvar Aalto dizzy. It goes without saying that their most notable works were produced in 1933–34.

While awareness of British plywood furniture was reawakened in the 1970s by academics, it did not have a splashy public airing until Abel and Ruby published their book in 2018. Because they deal in the material, too, they are effectively developing its market, but that is not what gets them out of bed each day. Obsessed by research, they are casting their attention on an obscure field whose time has come, at last, to be appreciated by a wider audience.

Meanwhile, they cast their attention on other disciplines, too. On a recent autumn day, I was alone in their living room, gazing at a view of turning leaves, slick with rain, as they prepared tea in the kitchen. All was quiet and still, except for the occasional clink or clank from the next room, and I felt a buzzing kind of peace familiar from childhood visits to my grandparents' house. Probably Abel and Ruby heard me cry out before I realized it myself. "THIS IS SO COOL!" An image had passed through me like an electrical charge. On the couple's coffee table, an inflatable PVC fruit bowl sat atop an antique lace doily. Nineties design was in vogue, but inflatables were largely unsung outside of fashion editorials and recondite zines. Lace was making a comeback among New Antiquarians, but I had never seen it paired with an industrial vessel like this. As Abel and Ruby began telling me about the objects, I marveled, for a few beats, at the magic of the combination.

Perhaps it is the fate of the young to give the pendulum of taste a shove every generation or so, just as it is the fate of every object that survives to become an antique. Happily these fates have combined in Abel and Ruby's practice, which celebrates old things even as it shows that they can remain, in an important sense, forever new.

Previous: While most of the objects in the parlor-slash-dining room date from the twentieth century, an abundance of natural materials, a focus on functionality, and a touch of lace on the mantel result in a timeless atmosphere. Among the modern icons in the room is an armchair designed by Gerrit Rietveld, a key reference for Abel. The folding stools by Barry Simpson, tucked beneath the bookshelves, are from later in the twentieth century. The inflatable fruit bowl by Nick Crosbie is from its closing days. Dean Edmonds's donut stool is contemporary, and not guaranteed to be comfortable.

To anyone foolish enough to think that modern things are immune from becoming antique, as if we have reached the End of (Decorative Arts) History, be warned: Rococo was considered a "modern" style in the eighteenth century, and a rocaille-enriched fauteuil was not designed to show its age any more than an Eames chair—or, for that matter, an installation by Donald Judd. Time cares not for makers' intentions, and history is greedy for objects. It comes for them all.

Right: A Czech modernist sofa, an imported Japanese chair retailed at Liberty & Co. around 1900, and an anonymous student painting seen in cool English light.

Opposite: In the couple's bedroom, a lone Fledermaus chair by Josef Hoffmann for Thonet resembles a museum display but could easily catch discarded clothing (and probably does, although I have never seen it). The Kerman carpet and pine wardrobe are antique, but the custom steel handles on the wardrobe by the couple's friend, furniture designer Dean Edmonds, gesture toward the present. At night, a Noguchi ceiling lamp elegantly filters the light of a single bulb.

Right: Serving as a nightstand is a painted stool by Alvar Aalto. A joinery sample by cabinetmaker Daniel Bradley cradles a copy of Peter Rabbit's *Drop City*, about a counterculture artists' community in Colorado that is said to have been the first hippie commune.

Above: A diminutive cast-aluminum figure is seated on a favorite stone, while an ancient Roman glass vessel is displayed as it might be in a museum, intensifying our awareness of the object's particularity—and our appreciation of its integrity.

Opposite: For New Antiquarians who rent their homes, vintage and antique objects personalize kitchens that might otherwise be coldly deracinated. Here, a shelf by Alvar Aalto holds a baffle lamp by Dean Edmonds and examples of Kralik glassware attributed to Koloman Moser. On the counter, the utensil pot is also by Edmonds. Take note that the labeled jars of dry goods and spices are not styled. Abel and Ruby, bless them, are alarmingly tidy.

XIII

EMILY EERDMANS

Greenwich Village, New York City

All things Mario Buatta, Lady Anne Gordon porcelain vegetables,
English Regency furniture, and illustrations by Jeremiah Goodman.

Anyone who assumes that traditional decoration must be tastefully conservative, or, worse, boring, does not know Emily Eerdmans. With the snap and fizz of a midcentury doyenne (pug dogs and exclamations of "darling!" in her santal-scented wake), she has yanked the realm of chintz and English antiques into the twenty-first century, first as an author of influential design histories, then as the architect of an instantly legendary, market-shaking series of auctions and estate sales following the death of her mentor, Mario Buatta, the interior designer widely known as the Prince of Chintz.

Credited with helping reawaken the taste for all things old, the Buatta sales are today referred to collectively (and deliciously) as "Buattacon," a name befitting their significance. As with all such cultural watersheds, Buattacon crystallized a zeitgeist that had been assembling itself in the background for some time, visible only to a few. Happily, like her mentor, who promoted the English country house look to a broad audience with the proselytizing zeal of a true believer, Emily proved to be a natural design evangelist, and she seized the nascent zeitgeist —a millennial return to bold, pretty, atmospheric decoration—with characteristic élan and a perfect sense of timing.

Like all good students, however, she is not content to regurgitate the lessons of the master, and to step into her home-slash-design gallery (yes, you read that correctly) in Greenwich Village (where else?) is to receive a jolt charged with the current of Emily's other idols: Madeleine Castaing, Nancy Lancaster, Sister Parish, and Henri Samuel, among other greats in the pantheon of twentieth-century decoration, all of whom she has researched with scholarly rigor, quite literally writing the book on most of her style icons.

To her credit, she refrains from channeling them in a doggedly literal way. In an era of two-dimensional decoration, rife with copy-paste imitations of particular designers or design tropes, Emily decorates in three dimensions, solving problems and creating atmospheres with a highly sophisticated set of tools. Chief among these is a vertiginously high level of connoisseurship, a distinction she shares with her heroes, who collected—and designed for collectors—as naturally as they breathed.

Knowing what things are—and, critically, being able to distinguish between "good, better, and best" examples of those things—was ironically easier in the past, when information may have been scarcer but the world it described was, fittingly, smaller. A scholar to her core, not to mention a certified appraiser, Emily embraces connoisseurial knowingness, elevating it to an art of its own and making it central to her practice as a writer, gallerist, and (increasingly) designer. It is her desire to share what she knows, however, that sets her apart from the design cognoscenti of yore and cements her role as a taste arbiter for our altogether more pluralistic era.

Attend an opening at Emily's gallery and you will see what I mean. After tripping in off the street, you will find yourself floating with sudden grace across leopard-print carpets and up a staircase lined with emerald-green murals in homage to Christian Bérard. At the top of the stairs, in a gallery encased with candy-shell chartreuse lacquer, you will behold a dizzying commotion of Park Avenue socialites, neighborhood regulars, former denizens of Andy Warhol's Factory, stray aristocrats, and Dimes Square ingenues venturing up from the Lower East Side in search of a truer, deeper kind of cool. Here they have found it. Primed by a revival of 1990s fashion, and ready to cast a whimsical eye on the predigital past, this latter group of visitors is perhaps Emily's keenest: New Antiquarians in the making. Emily greets them with open arms ("Darling!"), and it is only a matter of time before they are fluent in the finer points of Regency silver. Meanwhile, a few steps away, a wily octogenarian may well be livestreaming the encounter from behind a *secrétaire à abattant*.

To the untrained eye, material culture may seem to hold center stage here, but the cachepots and convex mirrors ultimately serve a deeper purpose: ready to be deployed in a thousand eccentric combinations, each object is destined to become a landmark in a complex personal landscape where individual taste, and thus imagination, enjoys free rein. As Emily's followers know, the results of this rare, heady freedom are anything but conservative, and they are never boring.

Previous: The front parlor is an homage to Emily's mentor, Mario Buatta, the "Prince of Chintz." An undulating sofa is covered in one of Buatta's favorite chintzes, Campanula, and the walls were drowned in aubergine lacquer by his longtime painter. Buatta believed fervently in bringing the garden indoors, and Emily has done just that with a 1950s floral still life by Jean Isy de Botton, vintage pillows hand-painted by decorative artist George Oakes, and a cheeky message in needlepoint.

Above: Antiques were made to be used. Here, an antique silver-plated tray holds television remotes and protects a Regency penwork table from Emily's husband, Andrew, a "Tasmanian devil."

Opposite: A Regency chiffonier is laden with a gardenful of Lady Anne Gordon porcelain vegetables, which Emily collects individually. The mirror above is one of her best things: English, circa 1780, and divinely attenuated.

Previous: Much of Emily's collection relates to the subjects of her books. Here, a surreal papier-mâché snail by Mark Gagnon recalls Henri Samuel's Paris salon for the d'Ornanos. Nodding to Buatta are the scarlet japanned bureau cabinet, decalcomania lamp, and silk cushion by George Oakes. The watercolor drawing hung above the cabinet, by Pierre Bergian, depicts Buatta's iconic, bow-bedecked living room. A peek into the kitchen, which is more than Emily allows most visitors, rewards the nosy with an antique porcelain conservatory cockatoo.

Opposite: In the bedroom, a panoply of patterns forms a surprisingly harmonious backdrop for Victorian shadow boxes of faux auricula, Buatta's favorite flower, and a George Oakes–painted vase that Emily glued to a bracket for her own safety (and that of her husband). Pro tip: museum-grade silicone adhesive is reversible.

Above: There is something wonderfully romantic—indeed, sentimental—about Emily's bedroom. In addition to a hundred inherited trinkets, including beautiful brushes and combs, there is a needlepoint pillow made by her mother in the 1980s, a watercolor of her friend Christopher Spitzmiller's geese, and a nineteenth-century Belgian oil painting of a lady with a little white dog that was a gift from her husband. He knew she wanted a dog, and now she has a real one, too: Pompey, a pug.

XIV

JARED AUSTIN

Harlem, New York City

Kashmir shawls, European printed textiles, Indonesian batik, vintage Bauer pottery, faience, art by Christian Bérard and Eugene Berman, bronze sculpture, and buttons.

In every small town in America there is a boy who covets old things, keeps collections in shoeboxes, and idolizes the women who stitch together the material world.

Some of these boys stay put and become florists, drapers, and drama teachers. Others board buses or trains bound for New York City, arrive in the warrens of Port Authority or Pennsylvania Station, and emerge into the city as men seeking their destinies. The unlucky do not survive. Others take up trades and ply the craft of beauty—and freedom—in their new home, where such things are practiced. Jared Austin is one of these.

He has lived in the same apartment on Central Park North for years, and every inch of his space is filled with meaning, intention, and collections. An interior designer at a firm whose billionaire clients are spread across the globe, Jared returns home to his things most nights, when he is not traveling, and tends to them with a fastidiousness that some believe is lost to our world. (It is not.) There are original works by Christian Bérard, one of his idols, and enviable collections of textiles, pottery, and more.

When I say "more," I mean to indicate vast but near-hidden collections amassed in the old way—that is, sequentially,

from one example to another within disciplines that hold the collector in a grip of fascination. The most surprising of these is Jared's button collection: a trove of vintage fasteners of every description, wired to sheets of paper by type ("Bakelite," "brass," "horn") with taxonomic rigor. While Jared has been exposed to the heights of the art and design worlds and has begun collecting "serious" material, this does not dim his enthusiasm for buttons. He inherited the practice from his mother, and the two intend to attend a button convention next year in Jared's home state of Oregon.

It was there that Jared set up a vintage clothing shop with his grandmother's help before making his way to Oz. Her influence can be seen in the riotously frilled floral curtains that line his living room, stitched up not from expensive polished chintz but a digitally printed lookalike produced on the cheap for use in saris. Fabrication of the curtains took one month, and the entire apartment was given over to the enterprise—a workroom scene that brings a wide smile to Jared's normally reserved countenance.

Another influence evident in the room, and particularly in those curtains, belongs to the legendary American design firm of Parish-Hadley, where Jared's design mentor was mentored in turn. Although Jared's scheme is wholly original (the curtains being an acid-trip riff on, not a copy of, classic chintz drapery), it evokes memories of Sister Parish and Albert Hadley in a family tree of design with deep matriarchal roots and flowering gay branches. It is difficult to imagine a more perfect setting for good vintage textiles and important fashion illustrations.

Jared's collection of vintage clothes remains intact in off-site storage, on his back, and in his closet. Happily there are no metaphorical closets in this story. Down the narrow, only-in-New York hallway, Jared's fabric-enrobed bedroom is a Stygian temple devoted to lush depictions of the male form. Nude bronzes grouped carefully on a bedside table could be assembled for a Spartan military exercise (or some other activity), and a 1970s Japanese sculpture of a glans penis sits beside the bed. Lengths of vintage Suzani and antique Kalamkari textiles, sourced from import boutiques and flea markets, hang from the upholstered walls. If Renzo Mongiardino were a millennial living in Harlem, this would be his bedroom.

On every block in New York is an aesthete hailing from elsewhere. Few collect with the proficiency of Jared, however, who has built a beautiful life for himself in collections. Without turning away from his past, they point toward his future, and to the rich possibilities for self-expression that a New Antiquarian can find in collecting.

Above: Although (or because) it is hidden in Jared's bedroom, this metallic altar to the male form is among the most compelling small-scale displays I have seen. Posing, fighting, and flexing bronze figures surround a pair of English candlesticks from the early nineteenth century. Their landscape is a twentieth-century French shawl scattered with seashells and objets. A dramatic backdrop is provided by a late nineteenth-century Kalamkari textile produced in India for the Persian market.

Opposite: Decadently layered vintage textiles absorb space and time, and Jared's bedroom feels as if it could be anywhere at any point in history. In fact, the room's objects mark time. The antique photo of San Francisco's Golden Gate Park ("Portals of the Past") belonged to Jared's great-grandparents, while the verdigris bronze figure of David was created by Raymond Delamarre around 1930. The ceramic lamp is French from the 1940s. Hanging above it are contemporary nude photographs by Daniel Handal.

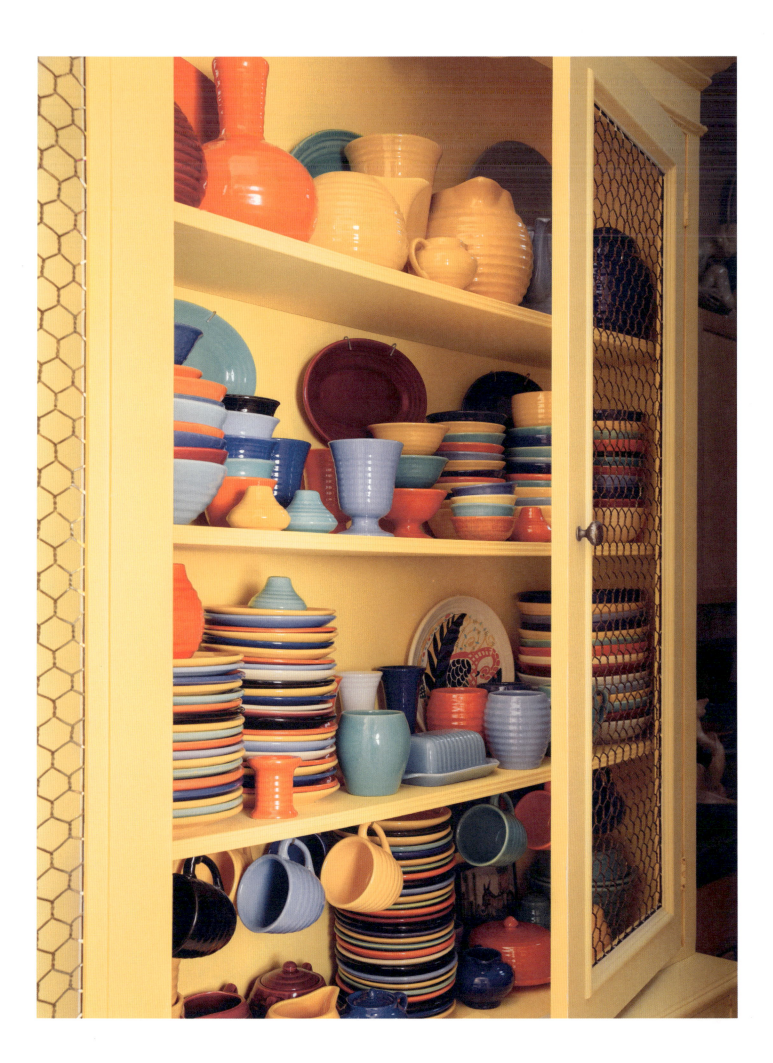

Previous: An interior designer by day, Jared pursues his collecting passion on evenings and weekends, assembling his jigsaw puzzle of an apartment over many years of auctions, estate sales, and buying trips abroad. The 1960s painting between the windows is by Eric de Kolb, perhaps best known for his jewelry designs, and indeed everything in the living room sings of fashion and the decorative arts. On the walls are midcentury works by Eugene Berman, to the left, and a 1946 illustration by Carl Erickson for Nettie Rosenstein, to the right. The ceramics on display range from a seventeenth-century Nevers faience plate to rippling midcentury vessels from the Vaga line by Wilhelm Kåge for Gustavsberg.

Sacrificing a weekend of estate sales, Jared sewed up the exuberant curtains himself—from a length of unpretentious chintz intended for saris.

Opposite and below: More than most of the New Antiquarians in this book, Jared has metabolized the tradition of collecting serially, and even obsessively, in highly specific disciplines. A chicken wire–fronted cabinet is filled with Bauer Pottery made in Los Angeles from the 1930s through the '50s. Buttons from Jared's extensive collection are mostly celluloid examples dating from the 1920s and '30s. At the time of writing, Jared was making plans to attend a button convention with his mother.

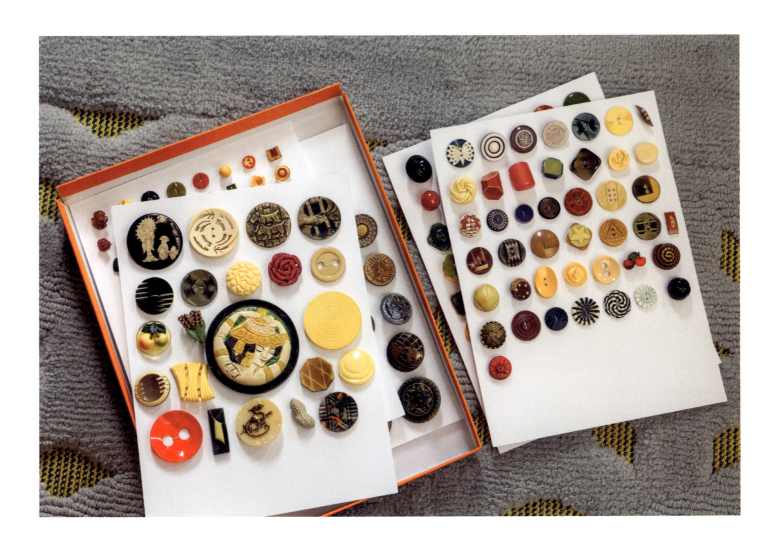

Above: A portrait of a beautiful young man, dated 1934, commands another altar to depictions of masculine physicality. Dating from the 1940s, the ceramic sculpture of Achilles is French. Despite the suggestion of a thematic focus, the vignette would not be Jared's if it did not include examples of the decorative arts from around the world. Here, the Art Deco chest of drawers by Widdicomb also displays a vintage Moroccan pot and nineteenth-century damascened steel doves from Qajar, Persia.

Opposite: All but two works on this wall are by Christian Bérard, a favorite of Jared's. They include original fashion illustrations for *Vogue*, theater and ballet designs, book illustrations, and a design for a screen.

XV

AVRIL NOLAN & QUY NGUYEN

Bushwick, Brooklyn

Modernity, simplicity, timelessness, execution, soul, geometry, and form.

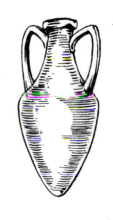

Suppose you were enjoying dinner at the home of a brilliant young couple you had just befriended. Much good wine was consumed, a fragrant fog hung in the air, and by dessert, their heads—instead of appearing as human heads normally do—appeared to take the form of geometric shapes: his, a sphere, and hers, a cylinder. Naturally you are startled, and you beat a hasty retreat, waving goodbye to the two queer figures and promising to return again soon. Indeed, you very much wish to do so, yet you find it difficult to leave in the first place, doubled up as you are—with laughter, and a touch of madness—on the sidewalk outside.

Reader, this happened to me, and I put the whole episode down to the particular brilliance of that young couple, Quy Nguyen and Avril Nolan, whose hospitality is matched only by their discerning taste in all things, including fragrant fogs.

Before we proceed, it should be noted that discerning taste, a good thing, is only a remote cousin of "good taste," a bad thing. Almost invariably, "good taste" tangles us up in received ideas, class prejudices, and all manner of narrowness best avoided by people with souls (that is you, Reader) or those wishing to appear soulful (whom we should pass over in silence).

The ability to judge well, on the other hand, carries us away from narrowness and toward expansiveness and encounters with the world's secret richness. With curiosity, patience, and the will to discern, you can easily identify the best of anything, understanding and comparing the intrinsic qualities of things. In these qualities, Reader, you will find surprise and delight. Your sense of what is best will be subjective, of course, and changing, but it will be related to what things are: dry, complex, dusty, florid. By contrast, "good taste" tells you nothing about things and everything about people. Left to select the best wine according to the standards of "good taste," you need only to understand the person sitting across from you.

Quy and Avril are uninterested in that person and have no time for moderately priced bottles of Sancerre. Instead, their interest is in things—and, particularly, objects—possessed of their own undeniable, if subtle, presence.

In their design showroom, Form Atelier, Quy and Avril obsess over quality, color, provenance, and endless other factors, but only if the essential form of a thing beguiles them. That thing could derive from any culture, genre, or era as long as it remains formally seductive when unburdened of its extrinsic qualities or extraneous details. Look around their atelier and you will see dozens of examples: A classical statue. A Shaker chair. A Noh mask. A live-edge table. Just as you are beginning to think it's all very sculptural, you will spy an Amish quilt, conceived with intense geometric rigor, folded gently in a corner.

Even the wall hangings in their atelier, riffing on a room by Renzo Mongiardino, bespeak Quy and Avril's fascination with form in its varied dimensions. Unlike traditional European draperies, awash in color and passementerie, these gently swagged panels are all about line. Approaching the zero degree of design to which pure white walls aspire, yet charged with formal interest, they could be from any place or time. Quy and Avril know precisely when and where they're from, of course, and they will giddily show you the Mongiardino reference over a glass of natural wine, but that reference is secondary to the enduring integrity—and interest—of a form distilled to its quintessence.

In a world of forms, Reader, you might suspect the air is quite thin. Not so in this one. As we arranged and adjusted the objects you see in these pages, I watched Quy and Avril work with what can only be described as joy. As we discovered visual connections between seemingly disparate things, the measure of joy increased, and the warmth of genuine happiness filled their atelier.

I was reminded of the evening, not long before, when I quaked with laughter (and a touch of madness) on the couple's sidewalk. *Whenever I am with them*, I thought, *like true connoisseurs, they expose me to the best things*. There is never any pretension, however, and even at its most sophisticated, their discerning taste always seems to be trained on that most innocent aim: pleasure, simple pleasure, in the world's secret richness.

Above: By separating objects in a strict grid, modular bookcases by Rud. Rasmussen paradoxically allow them to sing in chorus. Here, a Noh theater mask from the 1940s, a late eighteenth-century Wedgwood basalt vase, and a rare late eighteenth-century make-do pitcher form an unexpected ensemble. Empty cubbies beckon future acquisitions.

Opposite: Sharp contrasts are characteristic of Avril and Quy's visual Weltanschauung, but they are not the point of it. Here, a nineteenth-century Enfield Shaker chair rests against a partition hung with a print of the Witch Head Nebula by David Malin. A nebular vase by Svend Hammershøi, circa 1930, haunts the middle distance.

Opposite: When you bravely play with form, as Avril and Quy do, you may surprise yourself. Certainly I did when I helped the couple style this corner during a lunch break spent arranging objects for the sheer fun of it. Instead of thinking across periods or styles, we playfully considered color, texture, shape, and composition—the fundamentals of interior design, you might say, except there is no decor here. Every object is a treasure.

Above: When an ensemble of objects is drained of color, pure forms emerge. Instead of thinking about the history of this late nineteenth-century Parian ware figure, or the crackled glaze technique used to produce this 1970s ceramic egg by Pol Chambost, you could be forgiven for daydreaming about ovals, undulations, and the divine feminine. Unexpected dialogues are one of the pleasures of collecting like a New Antiquarian.

229

Above: Simple plywood shelves hold a Han dynasty earthenware figure, an early twentieth-century Chinese green glaze vase, and a 1930s McCoy vase in celadon green. Sometimes color is not the point. Sometimes it is everything.

232

XVI

SAMUEL SNIDER

Wiscasset, Maine

Homespuns, hooked and braided rugs, quilts, schoolgirl samplers, mocha ware, pre-1830 New England country furniture, wasp nests, and turn-of-the-century display cases.

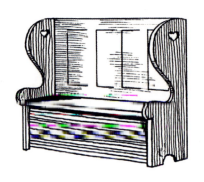

In another time, in another place, a young person in search of a new life might have boarded a ship to a distant land. Sailing into a strange port beneath an earth-straddling colossus, such a person might have looked up, inhaled the scent of unknown spices, and felt the terror and thrill of an entirely new life awaiting them on the approaching shore.

Today, in New York City, a young person in search of a new life might pack up their car and point it toward Maine. Driving into that strange state beneath a vault of pines, such a person might look up, inhale the sharp scent of the North, and feel the terror and thrill of an entirely new life awaiting them at the end of the highway.

Samuel Snider is just such a person. During the Covid-19 pandemic he gave up his Manhattan apartment, his fashion business, and his cosmopolitan métier and set off for a new life in the Maine woods. He had some advantages over the ancient traveler. Having spent a number of childhood summers in Vacationland, he was well acquainted with the state's special strangeness, not to mention its hard, cold beauty. He was acquainted, too, with the local inhabitants: antiques dealers. These soon became his mentors.

Today, instead of hustling in Babylon, Sam continues the great tradition of collecting—and dealing—that some have feared gone from this world.

News of Sam's existence reached me through one of his mentors, who is also a mentor of mine. "There's a new antiques dealer in Maine," the veteran dealer reported, as if a creature thought to be extinct had been spotted in the wild. Perhaps it had. "He's *young*." The word rang out, italicized, in the air, before an even more dramatic pronouncement was made: "He loves Americana."

By this point I had been tracking the New Antiquarians for years, and many of them (including myself) favored American art and material culture, which was undergoing a reevaluation: the manifold contributions of Black craftspeople were finally being recognized, and a fresh cycle of appreciation had begun for Shaker material, produced with unusually exacting rigor in a rational manner that could be seen, ahistorically but compellingly, as protomodernist. Strange and colorful examples of folk art were beginning to filter into Instagram feeds. Few new dealers had emerged in the field, however, and none were precisely *young*.

If you saw the clothing line that Sam produced in his city days, these words would not be needed. Reminiscent of nineteenth- and early twentieth-century workwear, his garments—stitched from unbleached linen, with curved hems and roomy work pockets—were a sartorial cri de coeur for simplicity, functionality, and a primitive kind of refinement. It is easy to understand why, in an era that favored streetwear and ribald eclecticism, he abandoned the business. It is equally easy to see why country furniture, antique tools, organic forms, and homespun textiles appeal to Sam, whose soul recognizes, and therefore demands as a requirement, the beauty of integrity. Why design anew and create waste when so many things of integrity exist already? Such questions emerge naturally in the clearing of a new life. Happily they do not need to be answered, only acted upon.

With the encouragement of his mentors, Sam acted. His home and shop, pictured here, follow loyally—which is to say, radically—in the New England tradition of collecting and displaying antiques, and Sam loyally—which is to say, radically—attends the regional antiques shows and country auctions his elders have frequented for decades. Recently we discussed the concessions at these events. Chili dogs and chowder, we agreed, are not millennial staples. While we may abstain from consuming them, however, we enjoy watching our mentors enjoy their naughty treats. Someday the food will suit us better, but something will be lost in the change.

As antiques dealers know: for one thing lost, another is gained, though never in quite the same form. Sam knows this, and, knowing his own mind, he is not shy about bringing new life to an old trade. He prefers material from the first quarter of the nineteenth century—a bit "late," believe it or not, in the context of early American furniture and folk art. And while I doubt he prefers social media to hooked rugs, pincushions, rocks, and moss, he does his duty as a young dealer and promotes his wares—and the practice of collecting—online, conducting quilt-washing tutorials and AMA (Ask Me Anything) sessions with candor and quiet verve.

Today, anywhere in the country, a young person in search of a new life might pack up their car and point it toward the source of those videos. Samuel Snider will be there, ready to receive the next generation of collectors just as he was received, and helped into a new life, not long ago.

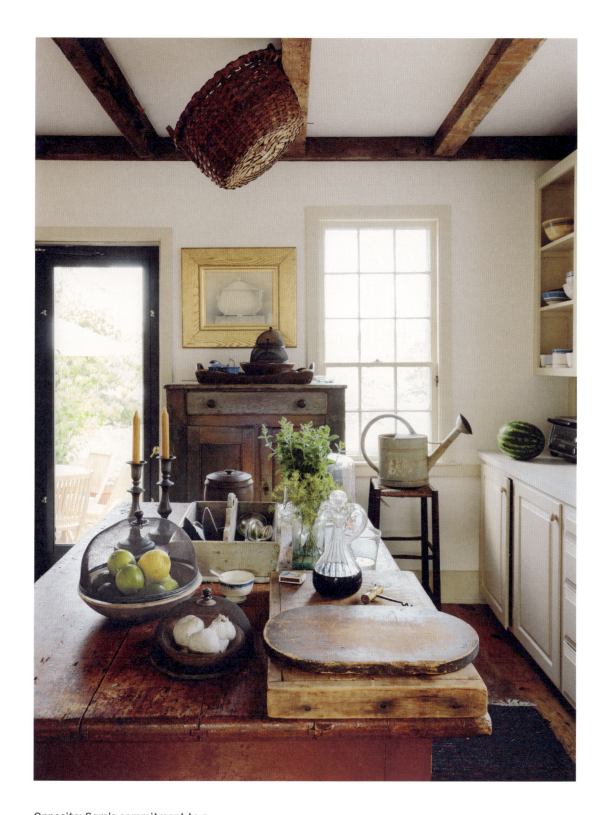

Opposite: Sam's commitment to a sustained practice of serial collecting is evident in his impressive collection of mocha ware and feather-edge Leeds creamware. Both types of pottery are perennially popular among Americana enthusiasts, and with their fresh, charming appeal on display in this nineteenth-century New England step-back cupboard, you can see why.

Above: For all the fuss over mixing antiques with modern and contemporary material, the purism of a period room remains peculiarly compelling. Imagine this one illumined only by candles and the spirit of youth. What could be more opulent? The textile mounted on the wall is an appliqué wool and velvet table rug from the 1830s. Every stick of furniture was produced in New England between 1800 and 1820.

Opposite: Within his collecting practice Sam favors humble objects, including schoolgirl samplers and other forms of women's work, rather than focusing on acknowledged masterpieces of design such as weathervanes. This New England schoolgirl watercolor from the 1830s hails from the collection of Robert Bishop, director of the American Folk Art Museum from 1977 to 1991, whose life was cut short by AIDS.

Opposite: Fitting within a hair's breadth of the ceiling beam in Sam's bedroom is an untouched Maine pencil post bed, circa 1830, with its original testers. Unusually, the netting is period. A nineteenth-century watercolor theorem hangs on the wall behind the bed, bestowing sweet dreams, and the antique log cabin quilt is in active use. Indeed, everything you see here is equally old, fresh-looking, and usable. Do not let anyone tell you that antiques are not for today.

Above: Three velvet strawberry emeries rest on a Leeds creamware platter encircled by pretty painted decoration. Used as pin cushions, the emeries once were functional objects. Now they are diminutive sculptures.

Overleaf: A view of Sam's antiques shop, which appears exactly as such a shop might have appeared fifty or even one hundred years ago.

XVII

ANDREW LAMAR HOPKINS

New Orleans, Louisiana

Paris porcelain, early Louisiana Creole furniture, eighteenth- and nineteenth-century Louisiana portraits, and items pertaining to Louisiana free people of color.

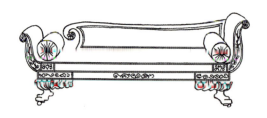

Andrew LaMar Hopkins may not have been Cleopatra in another life, but almost certainly he was French. That is what he thinks, anyway, and I am inclined to agree.

Not that he was born into Parisian splendor. As a boy in Mobile, Alabama, gay and Black and parched for glamour, Andrew found splendor in his television set, which piped in American Movie Classics and uncountable dreams of beauty: swashbuckling gentlemen, ladies adorned with door-busting wigs and panniers, and Rococo-inspired decors in black and white—or better still, Technicolor. When a commercial for Grey Poupon mustard interrupted the programming, he did not complain. Whatever was French was glamorous, and whatever was glamorous was good. At a time of life when most are operating lemonade stands, Andrew was sampling Dijon mustard and acquiring Old Paris porcelain with pocket change derived from the sale of historic room miniatures he modeled, with rigorous fidelity, in polymer clay. So what if the antique porcelain he collected was chipped? In time, he knew, he could afford better examples.

As adults we forget how agonizingly languid adolescence can be, like molasses dripping out of an upturned canister.

While Andrew awaited adulthood, he spent years in libraries, reading about neoclassical furniture and antebellum architecture, and he made sure to visit every historic house museum in Mobile. Instead of picturing him in their parlors, however, you must imagine him on porches and stoops, wincing as little white ladies in lace-curtained windows peered out at him, foolishly afraid of what they did not understand. Oftentimes injustice won and he was not welcomed inside. The days ticked by; racism held fast.

When Andrew's family moved to New Orleans, they might as well have moved to Versailles. The world cracked open like a bonbon. No historic house museum was off limits, and the doors of private homes flew open, too. Cosmopolitan New Orleanians welcomed Andrew into their historic preservation organizations, museums, and libraries, and soon he began appearing at auctions. As his connoisseurship skills grew, so too did his eyes. Before he could legally consume alcohol, Andrew was a hardened collector. The distinctions between "good, better, and best" mattered to him intensely, even if his own collection had only moved from "good" to "better." The best, he knew, would come.

At nineteen, in love with a Frenchman, he traveled to France for the first time. Recalling the journey now, he refers to French culture as *his* culture, as if it had always been so. And perhaps it was, all the way back through the centuries. The dream of beauty was as real in France as hard-paste porcelain, and he found the country's people to be unusually kind. Instead of shying away from him, little white ladies in provincial churches struck up attentive conversations, and the oppressive racial politics of the New World seemed far away. He felt, he says, like a whole person.

He remembered that feeling when he returned to New Orleans. Turning away from room miniatures and toward the painting practice he had begun cultivating at the age of thirteen, he took up the brush again. During all of those library visits he had learned about the free people of color living in Mobile, New Orleans, Savannah, and other Southern port cities during the nineteenth century. He had learned, too, that he was descended from free people of color—the first in a series of axis-spinning genealogical revelations. As he set to work, he sought to share the liberatory possibilities embedded in images of Black and mixed-race figures living in grand rooms, depicting nineteenth-century Creole society in faux-naïf renderings of quotidian life rich with historical detail. It is no accident that this allowed him to spend his working days with the historic architecture and material culture that circled permanently in his imagination. It is no accident, either, that his own collection provided him with numerous examples to draw and paint: pier mirrors, recamier sofas, Argand lamps, portraits of people of color, and hundreds of other objects. Only occasionally did he need to reach for a reference work. His own life had become one.

Today, Andrew lives and works between historic houses in the French Quarter of New Orleans and the city's Tremé neighborhood. By the time he learned that he was descended from a Frenchman who emigrated to the Gulf Coast in 1710, perhaps it did not matter as much as it would have once. Andrew knows his birthright now: an unapologetic créolité that pervades everything he does, whether he is performing in drag as Désirée Joséphine Duplantier (an extension of his art practice), painting an object from his collection, or collecting the thing itself—now, always, in the category of "best."

Page 251 and right: You may be surprised to learn that, in addition to the copious collections you see in these pages, Andrew owns several storage units full of material—including one in France. Here, however, is the opposite of storage. Andrew lives and works alongside the objects of his fascination, from signed portraits to flea market finds sourced in Paris. On the Creole mantel is part of the collection of Old Paris porcelain he has been assembling since adolescence. When you collect the material culture of the past, you collect stories, too—both from history and from your own life as a seeker of beauty and interest.

Below: A collection of mid-nineteenth-century daguerreotypes and cartes de visite from a family in Montgomery, Alabama, sit atop a seventeenth-century French tapestry fragment. The stray beads are exactly what you think they are. In New Orleans, the possibility of the carnivalesque is never absent.

Opposite: Throughout this book we have taken pains to show you how the New Antiquarians live, which means that we have rejected many of the tropes of "styled" interiors. Here, however, Andrew's fanciful tableau has been preserved. Why? Quite simply, this is how he lives—as if life were theater. Perhaps it is. Certainly this Louisiana daybed is dramatic. It was likely produced in the 1820s. Most of the paintings are French or American, and date from the eighteenth and nineteenth centuries.

Opposite: Andrew's painting studio is embedded in the intensely personal world he has built around himself. When a decorative arts reference is needed for a work, one is usually ready to hand nearby. Otherwise, he turns to reference books, photographs, and memory to provide the visual cues for his intricately detailed depictions of quotidian life in historic New Orleans. Walking around the city, he says, he often imagines what it was like two hundred years before. Sometimes, when he is not painting a known historical subject, he documents the kind of subjects that history forgot, or repressed—among them, discreetly queer encounters in beautiful rooms.

Below: On an antique table are arrayed the artifacts of everyday life in Andrew's world, including a miniature portrait by his own hand. An early nineteenth-century Paris porcelain tray produced by the manufactory of Pierre-Louis Dagoty sports a burnished gold border and a sepia scene derived from *Paul et Virginie*, the popular 1788 novel about life—including race relations—on the French-colonized island of Mauritius.

Previous: Instead of painting or papering the walls of his salon in Tremé, Andrew pinned up a length of paisley cloth. There could be no better backdrop for the early nineteenth-century American and European oil portraits on display. Below them is a carved French sofa and two American work tables of the same period. The table in the foreground is earlier (eighteenth century) and less urbane (hailing from Bordeaux) but no less beautiful.

Below: In Andrew's studio, pierced porcelain baskets hold Champagne corks, fans for overheated visitors, and the occasional work of art. Here the candles could be lit, and wine poured, at any moment. On the wall, a Creolized rendition of *The Birth of Venus* upends Botticelli's vision of love and beauty, replacing every figure in his composition with a Creole of color. The water is muddy, and Venus emerges from an oyster shell. Wildlife typical of the Gulf Coast greet her on the shore.

Acknowledgments

A pandemic, political upheavals, a cultural reckoning around race, and a personal brush with mortality stand between this book's beginnings in one era and its conclusion in what feels like another epoch altogether. Consequently, my thanks are due to a great number of people working in a wide range of fields, including medicine. To each person who propped me up (sometimes literally), rendered material aid to this project, or simply showed enthusiasm for it, I owe a debt of gratitude that can scarcely be repaid. I shall strive to do just that, however, in the hours that will no longer be devoted to producing the volume you now hold in your hands.

In particular, I should like to thank:

The New Antiquarians profiled in this book, who entrusted us with their homes, collections, and stories, and became a part of ours. I am forever grateful.

The New Antiquarians not highlighted in this book, who are many—and rapidly increasing in number. You give me hope, and I hope to chronicle your lives and collections next.

Seasoned collectors of all stripes, who showed the way.

My editor at Monacelli, Jenny Florence, an angel among mortals who keeps her wings tucked neatly away (but don't let her fool you). From our first meeting, Jenny was exactly the advocate this book needed in order to exist. Without her, quite simply, it would not. May it be the first of many.

Also, at Monacelli and Phaidon: Keith Fox, Philip Ruppel, William Norwich, Michael Vagnetti, Laura Mintz, Sierra Cortner, and everybody else who had a hand in conjuring my dream of making a book.

Alessandra Merrill, silver expert extraordinaire, who started it all with a thoughtful introduction.

The book's primary photographer, Brian W. Ferry, for being as kind as he is wise, and for sharing his talent so freely. It has been a joy to view the old things I love through his fresh lens, and to collaborate across disciplines in a spirit of open-hearted exchange—hopefully not for the last time.

Leon Foggitt, our photographer in England, who executed two quick-turnaround shoots with an unerring eye and flawless professionalism, thereby saving the day.

The book's creative director, Elizabeth Goodspeed, whose command of (simultaneously) the semiotics of ornament and open-source archival resources knows no equal in the field of graphic design, or indeed any field known to me. For each idea we implement, it seems, a thousand are filed for "next time." I suspect there will be many of those.

Abby Muir, for introducing me to Elizabeth (and much else besides).

James Brown and Ana Rita Teodoro at Cantina, who implemented the designs for the primary chapters with thoughtful rigor.

Benjamin Miller, another silver expert extraordinaire; host of the Curious Objects podcast for *The Magazine ANTIQUES*; and cofounder with me of the New Antiquarians, our affinity group for young collectors of antiques, historic art, and the material culture of the past (from which this title takes its name, with my gratitude).

Greg Cerio, Don Sparacin, Sammy Dalati, and all of my colleagues past and present at *The Magazine ANTIQUES*, which, having just turned one hundred years old, I hope to support through its next century.

Dara Caponigro of *FREDERIC*, Steele Marcoux of *VERANDA*, and Joanna Saltz of *House Beautiful*—visionary editors in chief who have believed in me, and, more importantly, who believe in a bright future for antiques and historic preservation. Thanks, too, to their staffs, and especially Emma Bazilian, Ellen McGauley, Tori Mellott, and Dayle Wood, who helped and encouraged along the way.

Special thanks, as well, to Michael Henry Adams, Julie Schlenger Adell, Annie Armstrong, Savona Bailey-McClain, Shayne Benowitz, Brian Boucher, Amanda Sims Clifford, Tony Freund, Jennifer Kelly Geddes, Cara Greenberg, Bebe Howorth, Eve Kahn, Gianluca Longo, Christopher Mason, Hannah Martin, Brook Mason, Johanna McBrien, Martha Moskowitz, Madeline O'Malley, Mitchell Owens, Clayton Pennington, Chelsea Retherford, Madelia Hickman Ring, Robert Rufino, Abby Shulz, and Greg Smith.

The indispensable Laura Beach and the indomitable Lita Solis-Cohen, for teaching me more about the antiques trade than I ever could have learned on my own. It strikes me that the fiercest custodians of our history are often the keenest advocates for the future.

Helen Allen and Lucinda Ballard, Executive Director and Co-Chair of The Winter Show, for being thoughtful (and tireless) leaders and dear friends. Many thanks as well to Michael Lynch, Tom Remien, Courtney Booth Christensen, all of my fabulous colleagues past and present on the Winter Show Advisory Council, and, in particular, my fellow Co-Chairs of Young Collectors Night—especially Lucinda May, a New Antiquarian to the core.

Arie Kopelman, for so clearly demonstrating the joy of collecting, and for helping me get my start (and keep going).

Patrick Bell, for everything you've given (and sold!) me, and for being family—a necessary presence in life, equally dependable during highs and lows.

Lucie Kitchener, Craig Brown, and Laura Archer, who honored the legacy of this book's dedicatee, Philip Hewat-Jaboor, with their Herculean work for Masterpiece London. Cheers, too, to my fellow former Co-Chairs of the Masterpiece Collectors Club. Onward!

Mark Rosen, Simone Stunz, and Cheyenne Wehren at TEFAF, and Magda Grigorian, who is with TEFAF but more importantly in my heart.

Gerald W.R. Ward, who demonstrated that connoisseurs are citizens, too, and should strive to be good ones.

Katie McKinney and Kate Carson Hughes, my sisters in the decorative arts.

Margaret Custer, for her care and constancy.

Lauren Byram, for the early exposure to "bow-bedecked big shirts," and abiding friendship.

Emily Adams Bode Aujla and Aaron Singh Aujla, who always make time for antiques and a good deed.

Camille Okhio, for suddenly being there, in the most wonderful way, as if she always was.

Andrew Nodell and Alex Rosenfield, brothers in life and laughter.

Bill Carpenter and Donna Gold, for teaching writing, and perhaps more importantly, for encouraging writing.

Jeff Nunokawa, for the gift of the essay.

Edmund Gordon and Andrew O'Hagan, for helping me understand the prose I wanted to write.

Richie Hofmann, for his song and support.

John Visvader, whose influence on my life (and therefore this book) is quietly pervasive.

Isabel Mancinelli, who helped me find the material world again after a break from it.

The Trustees of Sir John Soane's Museum Foundation, with the deepest gratitude for our time together and their continuing work.

Miguel Flores-Vianna, for offhandedly giving me the best piece of advice a person could ever offer.

Peter Sallick and Barbara Sallick, mentors in community, business, and books. It is an honor to be a part of their world.

My wonderful team at the Design Leadership Network: Meghan Buonocore, Brittany Cost, Julia Cotsarelis, Hadley Keller, and Ron Tumpowsky.

Ruth Mauldin, for her support through all of it.

Emily Eerdmans, for her friendship far beyond the bounds of any book, but also for her friendship in this one.

Ingrid Carozzi, whose flowers are outmatched only by her heart.

Betty and Dennis Balch, for their example.

The staff of NewYork-Presbyterian/Weill Cornell Medical Center, and especially Dr. Kelly Garrett, for everything.

Gavin Stamp, role model for all "young fogies," and a beloved mentor to this one, gone too soon.

Lt. Col. Robert T. Cumback, for the elements of style, and a jolt of early confidence.

Karen Waldron, who parented, taught, and mentored me, and who continues to do so whenever I appear on her doorstep, always with a permanently thrilling undertone of écriture.

Poorva Rajaram, for the years, and for being my lifelong referent for "criticality" as well as "best friend."

Sneha Rajaram, whom I once thought of as Poorva's sister and now think of as mine.

Usha Rajaram, my nickname for whom says it all: Amma. Many films flow silently through this book, which means that her spirit does, too.

And my dear family, whose support has made all the difference, especially:

J.E. and Duffie Griffith

Becky Wilkinson Perry and Jonathan Perry

Amy Smith Elashry

Lenny Rickards and Javier Platas Jaramillo

Jose Luis Díaz and Sandra Kleinburg

Diego Díaz Rickards and Lety Villegas Inman

Alejandra Befeler and Eduardo Befeler

Andy Griffith, my guide and source of daily wisdom, and Sherry Griffith.

Mary Ann Griffith, my dream-giver and permanent inspiration.

Brie Griffith, our future.

And Alonso Díaz Rickards, my beloved husband and partner in all things. But for you, there would be nothing.

Finally, thank you to everyone who loves old things, whatever your age. If you do not collect already, I hope this book inspires you to begin.

NOTES ON THE TYPE

Body Text: Henry by Matthieu Cortat (205TF)
Chapter Headlines: Albertus by Berthold Wolpe
Chapter Numbers: Top Tune by Jeff Levine
Script: Monte Cristo by Kevin Allan King and Patrick Griffin
Captions and Subheads: Styrene A by Berton Hasebe (Colophon)
Drop Caps: Goodwine by Gleb Guralnyk

Copyright © 2023 Michael Diaz-Griffith and The Monacelli Press

All photographs © Brian W. Ferry, except noted otherwise

Photographs on pp. 50–67, 176–89 © Leon Foggitt

All rights reserved. No part of this book may be reproduced, stored in a retrieval system, or transmitted in any form, by any means, including mechanical, electric, photocopying, recording or otherwise, without the prior written permission of the publisher.

Library of Congress Control Number: 2022948630

ISBN 978-1-58093-590-6

Design by Elizabeth Goodspeed and Cantina

Printed in China

Monacelli
A Phaidon Company
65 Bleecker Street
New York, New York 10012
monacellipress.com